UNREÁSONÁBLE

7 IMPACTFUL LESSONS DISCOVERED CLIMBING THE 7 SUMMITS

UNREÂSONÂBLE

7 IMPACTFUL LESSONS DISCOVERED
CLIMBING THE 7 SUMMITS

SCOTT R. CUTLAN

MBA, PM

DEDICATION

To those who recognize the boundless potential within and possess the courage to embrace it now.

I extend my deepest gratitude to the select few who have walked alongside us on this profound journey, offering support in ways beyond measure, the full extent of which we may never fully comprehend.

This book is dedicated to the skeptics, the disengaged, and the naysayers. It is a narrative meant for all, a call to approach its pages with open hearts and minds, embracing the inherent spirit of adventure that resides within each of us.

This journey is dedicated to those who have already embarked on the path of affirmation, who understand firsthand the sacrifices and unwavering commitment required to uphold their beliefs. You are intimately familiar with the challenges, the multitude of obstacles, and the relentless dedication demanded by saying 'yes.' I applaud your steadfast focus and unwavering pursuit of 'more.' Your determination to press forward in the face of opposition from individuals, organizations, and businesses is truly commendable.

Remember, your 'yes' not only transforms your own life but also influences those around you.

CONTENTS

FOREWORD
by David L. Reynolds

I have had the great pleasure of meeting many people from many walks of life. In my journey, I have met but a few who I find myself deeply challenged by the simplest of exchanges with. In fact, the number is two – one is my lifelong marital and life coach, and the other is Scott.

I was fortunate to cross paths with Scott through a common employer and was at once taken by his direct approach to problem-solving and his passion for sourcing, shall I say, interestingly weird people and journeys. His energy, grace, and purpose are captivating, even in the most mundane moments.

Unreasonable is an extraordinary account of his all-but-mundane journey to find existential meaning and purpose in climbing some of the most challenging and majestic mountains in the world. As each page turns, I am met with less emphasis on the actual climb, although wildly interesting, and introduced to the complex nuances of the interpersonal relationships it took to plan and execute each climb. The cultural and language barriers they overcome, the team relationships forged, and the physical, and often spiritual, sacrifices are honestly captured by Scott and become ubiquitous lessons applicable to the most abstruse circumstances.

You will be drawn to the rawness and grandeur of the adventure. You will also see method and order conflict and contrast with the messiness of the third world described in artful and conspicuous prose—a provocative bivouac to lands and altitudes foreign to most and deadly to others. As Scott returned from each climb, we would debrief over a cup of coffee, often for hours, and I could sense that I was witness to a transformation of spirit, soul, and mind. It was so powerful that it made me a bit uneasy. That uneasiness manifested in me, challenging my own sense of adventure and purpose, as I hope you do. How and where you show up matters, and *Unreasonable* will challenge that understanding.

INTRODUCTION

You should probably put this book down now. What I'm going to give you in these pages is *unreasonable*. It is going to challenge your thinking, your beliefs, and maybe your place in the world.

Most people spend their lives running from any challenge to their thinking or beliefs. This book isn't for those people. If that's you, let me save you a few hours. You can stop reading now.

I wrote this book for those who are open…

Those who are curious about all that is available…

Those with a sense (or even a knowing) that much more is available to us than what appears on the surface.

One more word of warning. I'm going to talk about God in this book. I'm going to talk about leadership. I'm going to talk about lessons I learned when I answered a call from God. You might think I'm crazy, and you might be offended. No apologies, but consider this fair warning. In the remainder of the book, I'm going to be direct about these matters. No beating around the bush to conform to our modern, watered-down culture.

Unreasonable

unreasonable[1]

adjective

un·rea·son·able ˌən-ˈrēz-nə-bəl, -ˈrē-zᵊn-ə-bəl

1: a: not governed by or acting according to reason

| *unreasonable* people

b: not conformable to reason : ABSURD

| *unreasonable* beliefs

2: exceeding the bounds of reason or moderation

| working under *unreasonable* pressure

The story you're about to read is unreasonable. The events, actions, and results are all *unreasonable*. As the definition above says, they are not governed by or acting in accordance with what we might commonly consider "reason" in our modern world. As Webster's Dictionary states, you may even find them *absurd*.

If, after my warning above, you're still reading, I'll assume you're open to considering things that, on the surface, appear unreasonable.

I've written this book for those leaders who know that nothing important happens if you're merely reasonable. Reasonable produces average. Unreasonable, when paired with the inner

---

[1] Miriam-Webster Dictionary; https://www.merriam-webster.com/dictionary/unreasonable. Accessed February 17, 2024.

knowing (faith) that more is available–*unreasonably more*–creates extraordinary connection, extraordinary understanding, and extraordinary impact.

Unreasonable Call

I was living the "American Dream" and had it all—a great, high-paying job with all its prestige. The ability to provide everything my family wanted. A beautiful, loving wife and kids. I had it all.

Yet, I felt unfulfilled. I traveled non-stop–separating me from family and friends.

I worked 20-plus hours a day, which disrupted my health and stopped me from being my best.

My employer, clients, and staff all had unrealistic expectations of me, and I began to strain under the weight of it all.

I knew more was available, but I did not know how to activate it.

It's common to believe we're not deserving or not good enough. Sometimes, we don't even realize there is more available to us when there actually is a lot more. I felt it, but I didn't know how to unlock a better way of being who I was meant to be.

What does "more is available" mean?

There is more abundance in the universe than we can even begin to perceive. Many people say they have an abundance mindset, and I believed that I was one of them before this journey began. I had no idea how much more is truly available to each of us. It took this trek to reveal it to me. Now, I'm able to share it with you.

In 2012, I began changing my mindset and sought out a stronger relationship with God. I met people every week, no matter where I was in the world, and established heartfelt connections. I call them God encounters.

Then, in December 2017, I felt deeply convicted that God was calling me to do four things:

Leave your job.
Climb the 7 Summits.
Start a Non-Profit.
Fund it yourself.

Every single one of those calls is *unreasonable!*

Who quits the kind of sought-after and high-paying job I had?

Few climb the 7 Summits.

Seems unreasonable to start a non-profit and fund it myself if I'm walking away from my source of income–my job.

Yet, I was convicted (not confident, not convinced…convicted) that I was to do these four things. I had no idea how or why. I just knew that this was the call.

> **Unreasonable Call**
>
> Genesis 22: ²He said [to Abraham], "Take your son, your only son Isaac, whom you love, and go to the land of Moriah, and offer him there as a burnt offering on one of the mountains of which I shall tell you."

Let's be candid. Most of the people I shared this call with thought I was nuts. This ask from God is so outside of what we consider normal and reasonable in modern culture that people simply couldn't wrap their heads around it.

I don't blame them.

Unreasonable Faith

It's one thing to receive an unreasonable call–from a boss, your wife, and yes, from God. It's quite another to lean in and respond in faith.

> **Unreasonable Faith**
>
> Genesis 22: ³So Abraham rose early in the morning, saddled his donkey, and took two of his young men with him, and his son Isaac. And he cut the wood for the burnt offering and arose and went to the place of which God had told him.

4On the third day Abraham lifted up his eyes and saw the place from afar. 5Then Abraham said to his young men, "Stay here with the donkey; I and the boy will go over there and worship and come again to you." 6And Abraham took the wood of the burnt offering and laid it on Isaac his son. And he took in his hand the fire and the knife. So they went both of them together. 7And Isaac said to his father Abraham, "My father!" And he said, "Here I am, my son." He said, "Behold, the fire and the wood, but where is the lamb for a burnt offering?" 8Abraham said, "God will provide for himself the lamb for a burnt offering, my son." So they went both of them together. 9When they came to the place of which God had told him, Abraham built the altar there and laid the wood in order and bound Isaac his son and laid him on the altar, on top of the wood. 10Then Abraham reached out his hand and took the knife to slaughter his son.

That's crazy, right? People didn't believe this was a smart thing to do, but I was caught up in the strength of the call He placed upon me. I was inspired to take action, cause a disruption, and do the unthinkable.

I chose to say YES and take that leap of faith into the unknown. My YES led me on a journey that was risky but also exhilarating and beautiful.

Unreasonable Abundance

Saying "YES!" to the call meant risking my livelihood, my family's security, my reputation in business, many of my relationships, and yes, even risking my life. It all had to be released–placed on the altar to be sacrificed–to fulfill the call.

> **Unreasonable Abundance**
>
> Genesis 22: [11]But the angel of the LORD called to him [Abraham] from heaven and said, "Abraham, Abraham!" And he said, "Here I am." [12]He said, "Do not lay your hand on the boy or do anything to him, for now I know that you fear God, seeing you have not withheld your son, your only son, from me." [13]And Abraham lifted up his eyes and looked, and behold, behind him was a ram, caught in a thicket by his horns. And Abraham went and took the ram and offered it up as a burnt offering instead of his son. [14]So Abraham called the name of that place, "The LORD will provide"; as it is said to this day, "On the mount of the LORD it shall be provided."

My willingness to sacrifice those things that I had come to value so much opened up opportunities to experience true abundance in its many dimensions (as you'll discover with me on each of the climbs).

When I began this journey in 2017, I didn't even know what the 7 summits were. I was not a mountain climber. I didn't know where to begin or why I was being asked to take this trek.

Along the way, God gave me a specific word for each summit. My experience getting to and climbing each mountain revealed the meaning and significance of each word. Each word builds upon the ones before it and is a path for transformation. These words have become a roadmap to create positive change in my life, my family's life, and that of others around the world.

As you read this book, I encourage you to be open to two questions:

1. What are you being called to do?
2. What's holding you back from doing it?

I don't know why I was called to this particular journey, and I'm confident that most of us are not called to go to the ends of the Earth. That does not diminish your call. In fact, the most important calls are those to everyday leaders who spread love and create impact where they are.

Are you ready to open up and lead people with a servant's heart and a passion for the well-being of those around you?

Let's go!

CHAPTER 1

Kilimanjaro - Remember Your Purpose

*"He pursues them and passes on safely,
by paths his feet have not trod."*
Isaiah 41:3 (ESV)

Purpose is clarity about *what* you're supposed to do.

When you choose to say "yes" and take the unique journey God calls you to, you will not understand. As I write this, it's hard to go back to where I was mentally at this beginning stage of the journey. I had no idea why He called me to climb mountains. I had no idea what I was supposed to do, except climb these mountains, start a non-profit, and fund it myself.

I didn't know where to even begin. Which mountain should go first? What will the non-profit do? And, I just quit my job, how in the world will I fund the non-profit myself?

I want you to pause for just a moment as you're reading and let those questions sink in. What would you do when faced with that level of uncertainty? Put yourself in my shoes for this moment. You're me. What do you feel? How do you think you'd respond?

How Do You Climb a Mountain?

One step at a time…

I started my research of the 7 Summits. My friends and former colleagues were skeptical. Some were even hostile to what I was doing. I understood why. Saying out loud that you're called by God sounds crazy in our modern American/Western culture. Acting upon it by leaving a successful job, leaving my family for weeks or months at a time to climb mountains, starting a non-profit, and then funding it myself…it is crazy by our cultural standards of behavior.

It was hard to hear the criticism from people I cared about. When you've achieved a level of status and credibility within a community or industry, like I had, giving it up is hard. Some thought I was certifiably nuts. Others thought I was acting selfishly, putting the weight of the family on Melanie, and leaving the boy behind while I chased my windmills. I think the hardest to reconcile, though, were my friends in faith who suggested that I created the call in an attempt to have God bless my plans, versus following His plan for me.

My time in prayer was spent building up the courage to push back against the doubts.

Through prayer, Melanie and I understood otherwise—that He was clearing a path before us that we had to follow. I had to climb the 7 Summits for something bigger than we ever imagined, and that gave me the courage to step on the plane to my first summit: Mt. Kilimanjaro in Tanzania, Africa.

Step 1: Leaning on Faith

Kilimanjaro is a volcano—the tallest mountain in Africa. If you're unfamiliar with Kilimanjaro, it is near the eastern coast of Africa—212 miles south of the Equator and 174 miles from the Indian Ocean.

Of the 7 Summits, Kilimanjaro is generally considered the most approachable for inexperienced climbers. It is more like a hike to the top than a highly technical climb, which is why it attracts 30,000 climbers, supported by 80,000 porters, each year. It is the safest among the summits–with an average of just ten deaths on the mountain per year out of the 110,000 people who climb.

Now that I knew which mountain I would climb first, I had to take a leap of faith to say "yes" and trust God.

While I have traveled a lot in my career, this was different. I'm a dedicated planner. When I travel, every detail, down to every location, hour, and activity, is planned out before I arrive. With Kilimanjaro, it was all faith. I couldn't plan out every detail. I didn't know what to expect... I was flying 10,000 miles away from my family to the other side of the world, with no understanding of what I was getting myself into on this climb.

I did not understand why I was called to climb mountains. I leaned on being obedient through the doubts of others who challenged my conviction. The path we are meant to follow isn't always the same path the world wants us to follow. I had to trust that what I needed would become available when I needed it.

I'm no stranger to mountain hikes. I live in the Colorado Rockies. I hike in the mountains often. Focusing on familiar physical preparations helped me feel more in control and maintain the courage to continue. Since Kilimanjaro required less technical skills to climb, it felt like the right place to start.

Stepping Into the Unknown

While planning for this climb, I tackled my doubts. My climbing experience up to that point was little more than recreational hiking in the Colorado mountains. I didn't fully comprehend all the logistics and plans necessary to climb a mountain. I found it frustrating to not be able to get to the climb right away. I felt I was in good enough shape to simply walk up the mountain.

There was so much I didn't understand about the requirements...
Why did I need porters?
Why do we waste time involving so many other people?
Why do climbers go to all this expense?

I share all of that because this is the common experience when we're asked to do anything new, difficult, and far outside our comfort zone. We are confronted with the unknown, which brings fear, anxiety, and doubt. Those are all normal human reactions. The question is, what will you do with those reactions? My answer was to trust God.

I'm no saint, and it wasn't easy. I'm the type of person who just digs in and gets things done when I know the goal. I focused on trusting God to stay as calm and patient as possible, even though it is against my nature.

Before I left, I prayed for guidance. I gathered a group of people I trusted who would help me develop the New Reach Foundation—my non-profit. Like most startup organizations, there was plenty of excitement and more than our share of chaos and unknowns. We had no idea what this new organization would do. We didn't yet have clarity about the organization's purpose, yet we had a laser focus on the reality that He was guiding us.

I held on to faithful obedience and set out to follow His instructions—to climb this first mountain.

Overwhelming Uncertainty

Tanzania proved to be a challenging place to get to, and I learned to expect setbacks. I arrived at Jomo Kenyatta International Airport in the middle of the night, only to discover my bags were stuck in Zurich. With help from the right people, my gear arrived the next day, and I headed to Tanzania.

I struggled with doubts in my training. Back at home, I did the best I could. I worked out, hiked, and ran during the months leading up to the trip. I felt I was in good shape, but I didn't know if it would be enough.

Spiritually, I started seeking answers from God. Through prayer, I asked the questions: "What does this mean?" and "Why am I here?" The unknowns made me uncomfortable, and I attempted to gain control by seeking answers before I embarked on the climb.

Our journeys are full of micro experiences that lead to other opportunities. My search for an expedition company to help me climb this mountain led to one of those experiences.

I landed on a company that uses people local to the mountain. More importantly, they treat them properly.

I found a company that provided excellent guidance and added a sense of security to the climb. The idea of prepping and knowing what gear you need on these trips is overwhelming. Knowing how and what to pack takes a different way of thinking, and their guidance helped me get it right. It allowed me to be the most prepared of the group and to assist others by letting them borrow some layers. God provided what I needed through them and gave me a great experience that led to a long-term relationship with this company through the New Reach Foundation.

Discovery of Community

I've traveled all over the world for work, but on this trip, in the heart of Africa, I saw people differently. The locals moved in unison at the base to help guide us, weighing everything and ensuring all restrictions were met. Things began to click for me as I felt the love of this community in how they engaged with us and one another. This was their world, and their community derived its livelihood from the people who came to hike the largest freestanding mountain in the world.

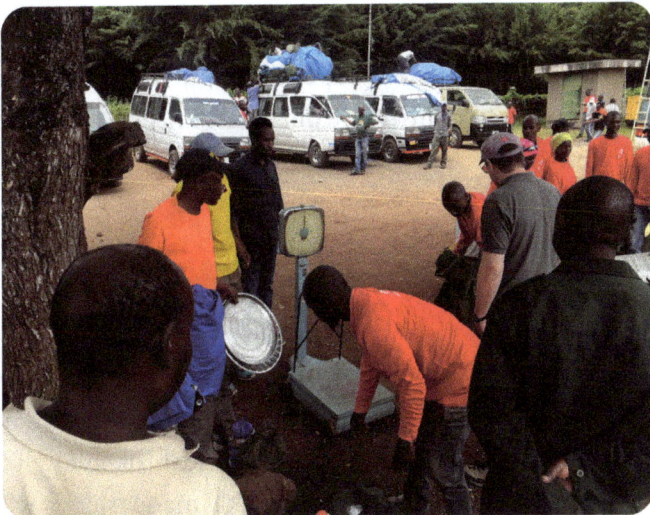

At that point, I stopped questioning everything and fell completely in love with these people, their communities, and their culture. This wasn't like the one-day hikes I was used to. Kilimanjaro is a respectful climb with real altitude that can take a week or more, depending on what route you choose. Taking the time to truly see these people made me see how it really does take a tribe to move along this mountain.

Sometimes, we are so inwardly focused on our own thoughts and our need to be independent that we miss the important messages in front of us. We forget to value the people and communities around us that make our work and life possible. Africa opened my eyes to how climber support allows the communities around these mountains to thrive. It's not perfect. There's a lot of abuse among the Kilimanjaro people. With every trip, I intentionally plan things so they make a positive impact by choosing companies that use local teams and that make sure they're treated properly.

Being exposed to the community around Kilimanjaro provided a first and important lesson. I spent too much time focusing on myself and trying to control the outcome. I needed to let go and trust in Him.

Approaching the Climb

Once all our gear was weighed in, we began to hike. My mind was wide open and ready to learn more about what it takes to climb this mountain. Even though they spoke broken English, the locals were easy to get along with. I quickly made friends with the guides, especially Emmanuel, the lead guide. Whenever a sliver of doubt entered my mind on this climb, he seemed to appear magically, his infectious smile and love for the mountain moving me to stay focused on the beauty around us and within us.

I also chatted with climbers from Dubai, Israel, and South Africa. I learned more about their cultures as we exchanged stories of our homes. We soon hiked into a flurry of activity at First Camp. Through the bustle of activity and tents, I met people from all over the world and all walks of life.

I soon discovered that the climbing world is small, and I embraced that moment. People from all over the world came together with this one common goal. Why are they here? What drives them and all these things into motion?

The mountain climbing world can be lonely, isolated, and self-motivated. People tend to focus on *their* equipment, *their* conditioning, and *their* goals. These people connect over an activity they spent months training for. It's easy to get focused inward.

And here we were in a camp surrounded by a rainforest full of Blue Monkeys. I mean, they were everywhere, entertaining us, and I guess we were entertaining them, too. Climbers were pumped up for an adventure with so much joy, happiness, struggle, challenge, and camaraderie.

Becoming part of the mountain climbing community was a huge learning experience for me. I was still working on learning how to let go and give this journey to Him. To stop trying to control the outcome of what He asked me to do versus just being in it.

You're Strong Enough

Even as God was using this mountain to work on my heart and prepare me for something greater, I was still in a world I knew nothing about. Previously used to one-day hikes, a multi-day expedition was a huge adjustment. Climbers go through many highs and lows brought on by lack of nutrients, weather, team morale, and other factors. We were on the move for hours at a time, giving us time to think and be in our own headspace.

Uncertainty and doubts crept in. I kept telling myself that He made me in a way where I was just strong enough to do it. I was adequate.

Building relationships with other climbers and the locals helped me keep going. It's easier to meet the challenges laid before you when you have others to share it with—especially when you learn just how dangerous some challenges can be.

Kilimanjaro is about more than just what they advertise. They keep news about people dying on the mountain or the struggles under the radar. It happens. During our climb, we witnessed local people getting blinded or losing legs and their ability to work for their families. The locals sacrifice everything for their climbers, especially when those risks stack up because climbers get summit fever or are not as aware of the dangers as they should be. Yet, they're so honored to work for us with a selfless servant's heart. They want to be there, and you're just falling in love with these people on the way up.

There's a huge lesson we can learn from that. I've observed numerous instances where team members are spoken to disparagingly as if their compensation warrants such treatment. How does the dynamic within your team unfold in such interactions, whether they are new hires or from different cultural backgrounds?

Anything's Possible

When you're pressed, the real you comes out.

When you heed God's call to find your purpose, it's like when you squeeze an orange. The orange is pressed to release its nutrient-enriched juice. Likewise, your unique path will squeeze the best out of you if you trust the journey. God knows what you're capable of and that you can handle the pressure. Your purpose will lead you to accomplish something extraordinary.

On this Kilimanjaro climb, a young girl on the team worked for an NGO in South Africa. She was not in shape for the climb, and as we continued the trek, she became slower and slower. The African leaders could have sent her back, but they refused to give up on her. As I watched them physically push her up the trail, their need to help this person succeed and their determination to not let her give up on herself moved me.

What kind of an impact could each of us make if we were as invested in the success of others as they were?

Pole, Pole

On the mountain, we're in the unknown, striding for that purpose. It's pretty darn uncomfortable when you're surrounded by so many unknowns. You must learn to let go of trying to control the outcome. I was still trying to learn how to let go of being in control at this point.

I was super excited to reach a personal record altitude of 4,600 meters/15,387 feet on day three when we stopped at Lava Tower. They, of course, told me not to climb up the tower. And, of course, I climbed it as high as I could anyway and just sat there, taking in the breathtaking environment.

I felt undeserving, still with no idea why I was there. At the same time, I felt honored and excited to be at that point. God had everything under control. My purpose would become clear, and its greatness would move me toward the next big thing. Peacefulness swept over me as I accepted this gift from Him.

When we moved on, the leaders taught us about the flowers and the nature around us. They also taught us a Swahili term. *Pole*. *Pole* means to move slowly. They also said, "Hakuna Matata." Don't worry. It's good. It's all about the concept of moving slowly.

Living life in the business world, we get used to moving fast, not thinking, and letting our expertise take over. Learning how to slow down when possible and acclimate to the challenge before us broadens our awareness. Moving slowly sometimes makes us stronger. *Akuna Matata.* It's all good. You're preparing for something big.

At the Barranco camp after the Lava Tower, we're in this huge expansive area that allows you to see over Africa on a clear day. It's absolutely beautiful.

We are above the clouds, and there's a thunderstorm. It's raining below us, and we're sitting above it. You could hear the storm, the rain. You could almost see it.

It's an odd experience. In the Colorado mountains, we're taught never to hike or camp in lightning and thunderstorms. Yet, here I am, sitting right on top of one.

Focusing on the Summit

Reaching the point where you can see your end goal can be intimidating. For us, it was the Barranco Wall. The Barranco Wall is over 800 ft high, and you scramble diagonally up and across the face of the mountain. It doesn't require technical climbing skills to get through. It's also not a walk in the park.

Tensions among the climbers mounted as we approached this part of the climb. We had to use all four limbs to ascend, occasionally putting one foot carefully in front of the other to avoid falling. I really enjoyed this exhilarating part of the climb, and others discovered it wasn't as difficult as they anticipated.

At the top, we reached a flat area, and my team convinced me to pull out the banner I had brought along to launch the New Reach Foundation. The shot was perfect, as the mountain silhouette on the banner looked like the vantage point of an actual mountain. It's pretty cool how things just seem to work out right when you keep moving forward.

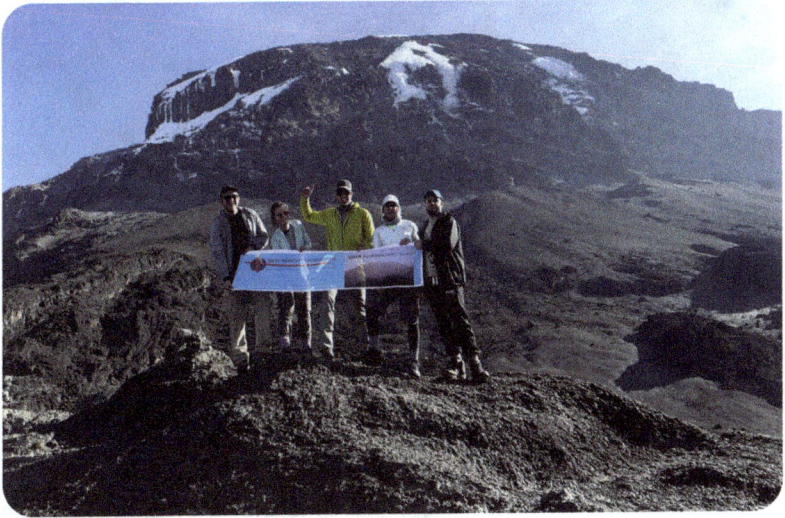

We didn't know what New Reach Foundation would focus on at that point, but we knew we were starting something big. This moment became another thrilling unknown He was leading me into as part of my conviction to follow His call.

Everyone became hyper-focused on the summit after that. We were getting closer. People were reaching the point of physical and mental exertion. The urge to rush forward to the summit intensified.

But still, it's *pole, pole*. Take your time. Enjoy it.

Mountains are Unpredictable

After the Barranco Wall, we were told that a snowstorm was coming. I didn't think it was a big deal, but a few other climbers became worried. I'm from Colorado, and I've been in my share of snowstorms on mountains—I wasn't concerned. Soon, I learned just how ignorant I was of the danger of a snowstorm on *this* mountain.

Blizzards while climbing on Kilimanjaro are a lot different than blizzards in Colorado. This was supposed to be a new experience, an approachable climb easy to learn how to summit. This weather wasn't just unexpected. It was highly unusual for Kilimanjaro.

Two days later, the storm hit. It got bad, so bad that we had to take an alternate way up instead of the usual route. The snow was up to our hips, but something else distracted me from the weather. This was my first exposure to real altitude. I didn't know if my body could handle altitude sickness. You never know. Some of the best climbers in the world can't be at altitude.

It's *pole, pole*. We took a step and a couple of breaths, and a step and a couple of breaths. Now, everyone's focused on the summit. The high altitude is affecting us. We're feeling physical and mental exertion at a high level at this point, but we are excited. We're really going to summit. We can almost feel it. Just a little further. Fighting the urge to rush forward is difficult when you're so close to your goal.

A storm this intense is unusual on Kilimanjaro. We lost two of our guides who left the main group to help other members of our team who could not keep up.

Joseph, our assistant guide, had an especially hard time. I was behind him and caught him when he fell. Through the wind-blown snow, he nodded his thanks to me, and I caught a glimpse of worry in his eyes. This is a guy who does this all the time and these conditions caused him to fall. The revelation added a sliver of worry to my own feelings.

Our bodies react differently at high altitudes, and man, I felt it then. The movement I made to catch Joseph knocked the wind out of me. It took us both a few moments to recover. Even then, it left me with one of the worst headaches. And then, Joseph fell a second time within a matter of ten minutes. It took all my focus and effort just to concentrate on pushing through it. I didn't know what else to do.

By the time we reached Stella Point at 5,756 meters/18,859 feet, the world around us was dark, windy, and just a mass of snowy chaos. Blinding whiteness engulfed us. The wind wailed around us, whipping icy shards of snow at us. But the fact that we were almost to the summit pushed us forward—until we saw the men in front of us.

A line of Africans stood with their arms out, blocking the pathway to the summit.

Nobody's Going to the Summit

The weather had turned so bad that the ranger station sent people to stop us from going further. We were close to the top and had been through much to reach this point. We didn't care. The summit was only 139 meters/456 feet higher.

The deep snow and probably negative 30 degrees Fahrenheit threatened us with frostbite. It was way out of the norm for Kilimanjaro throughout the year. I mean, way off. It was an anomaly. I was absolutely frustrated. People were confused, fear evident on their faces.

I was shaken, disappointed, and mad. It wasn't supposed to go this way. My deep feeling was, "I'm going at all costs. Get out of my way."

Then there was that pause. I caught myself and mentally zoomed out of my body. My point of view was above, and I saw what was happening. It was absolute chaos. People were throwing up. Many were delusional and being rushed down the mountain. My friend from Israel was suffering from Acute Mountain Sickness (AMS). His eyes were all googly-eyed, and Joseph ran him down the mountain. It was the first time I witnessed someone with AMS.

> **Acute Mountain Sickness**
>
> Our bodies undergo physical distress from adjusting to lower oxygen pressure at high altitudes. Some climbers have difficulty with this. Most cases are mild, but some can become life-threatening.
>
> Symptoms include headache, nausea, shortness of breath, dizziness, vomiting, and fatigue. Climbers suffering mild reactions to the high altitude adjust, and the symptoms often lessen in one to three days. Climbers with severe AMS may require oxygen, medication, and assistance moving to a lower altitude.

I remember my friend saying later, "Why would anyone want to go through this? It is horrible. I am not going to die and leave my family." Yes, even on Kilimanjaro, things go wrong and get bad.

It's like trying to ride out a turbulent sea during a storm in a pitching boat. Waves crashing, winds howling, and everyone is panicking trying to lash everything down and keep things from flying overboard, including themselves. It's uncontrolled chaos. That's what I saw on that mountain.

For some reason, I felt very calm. I focused on Jesus and thought, "What would Jesus do?"

> It's during situations like this that He gets down to where we're at. He puts his arms around us and gets us through these things.

In that intense moment, I realized this climbing journey wasn't really about my summit. It was about helping other people get down. My path to purpose and greatness was in meeting people where they were at and helping them. I had a choice. I could sit in frustration and bask in the failure of my summit or step up and do the right thing.

I made a decision to help my team and some others get down. I literally put my arms around their shoulders and focused on getting us down the mountain. We didn't have a guide at this point. They needed help, and I needed to step up and take care of these people. This is the simple nature of what Jesus would do.

Descent Doesn't Mean Failure

I took that lead role and brought the team down. There should have been an assistant and helper in the back, but he ran off. I had plenty of prayer time while working through the frustration. I would have to come back. I'm going to have to do the summit. I didn't want to spend the money. I didn't want to take the time.

I entered the victim mentality—poor me.

As we moved back down the mountain, I toggled between being a victim and knowing I was doing the right thing. That's good, right? Those feelings were real. We must acknowledge all our emotions and moments, both good and bad.

I knew and was comfortable with one fact. This is what our King would do. This is what we're supposed to do in living the life we choose to live. This is the right thing.

The Defining Moment of Failure

We made it back to the Barafu Base Camp, the high camp at 4,673 meters/15,333 feet. It was time to start gathering our things and head down out of the mountain. It was our defining moment of failure.

Everyone wanted to summit. Everyone faced the failure to summit amid adverse weather conditions. We got up high. We fought a battle. It was challenging and hard, but none of us hit our goal. None of us summited.

Every individual was riding an emotional roller coaster while packing up. We planned to head down the mountain to a specific camp for the night. We were walking out the next day.

Things Often Don't Turn Out as We Expect

About a thousand feet below Barafu Camp, Emmanuel turned to me and pointed to where I had the New Reach Foundation banner stuffed in my pack. I had nearly forgotten about that important part of my summit mission. He got in my face, shook his finger at me, and said, "Your logo is important. You want to go to the summit?"

In that moment, the spirit filled me. "Yes, I want to go."

Emmanuel snapped his fingers, and a flurry of activity followed. Porters brought over tents and set them up for us on the side of the trail in the snow. Some smiled encouragingly to me, while a few others had a worried look in their eyes behind their smiles. We had some soup while we recovered enough to go back up the mountain. I could see the thrill of anticipation and determination reflected back at me through Emmanuel's encouraging smile as we left.

The mountain weather grew worse as we started back up the mountain. Tired and frustrated climbers came down as we went up. We passed by those injured, people being assisted through broken legs, snow blindness, and even death.

Emmanuel and I focused on moving up, climbing in unison. We were fighting a battle together and forming a long-lasting relationship. It was beautiful. Through it all, the weather continued to worsen, and people continued to come down as we pushed through.

We summited, meeting the one other person who managed to persevere through the worst that nature had ever thrown at Kilimanjaro that day. I felt an intense sense of accomplishment and bonded with Emmanuel that day in a way I never expected. That friendship became the precursor to the relationships our foundation has built to make important impacts around the world.

It normally takes around two days to descend Kilimanjaro. You travel approximately five hours to reach camp and then four to six hours the next day. We pushed through it and arrived at the hotel one hour after the rest of the team.

They called me the strong American lion in Swahili, *simba wa marekani mwenye nguvu.*

The Stamp of Purpose

That's how He put the word *purpose* on Kilimanjaro. He clarified it at that moment when I chose to meet those people where they were at. I was confident in knowing who I am and who He made me to be. He opened me up and allowed me to live for the other people around me.

My Purpose is About Other People

I made a conscious choice to let my inside feelings go and do the right thing. These pivotal moments would not have happened if I had not been willing to sacrifice my goal. All I had was my step of faith. I didn't have the proper preparation in place. I didn't have the right training or the right mindset, but I had the relentless pursuit, and I learned to let go—to stop trying to control the outcome. It was all Him.

Most people go on this journey inwardly focused on themselves when we're really called to go on the journey selflessly. With purpose, you understand what you're supposed to do and how you're supposed to do it. Choosing to live out your purpose will positively impact individuals, communities, and cultures. There's nothing else like it.

Purpose helps you discover your *Greatness*. Greatness is the goosebumps moment of striving in that purpose—of living it and being alive. These experiences elicit emotions so strong that they reach a level of intensity that triggers goosebumps. It raises your hairs on end and moves you to tears. Seeing others in their moment of greatness is extraordinary.

My purpose began to take form while preparing to go to Africa. I attempted to maintain control through countless meetings, and everything I tried to set up ahead of time was 100% failure. Too many unknowns intervened. However, I realized after the climb that everything was perfectly aligned. Those were the moments meant to happen. Those conversations, moments, and relationships all happened for a reason.

When you release control and take a step of obedience, things fall into place. Just be who you are and take action.

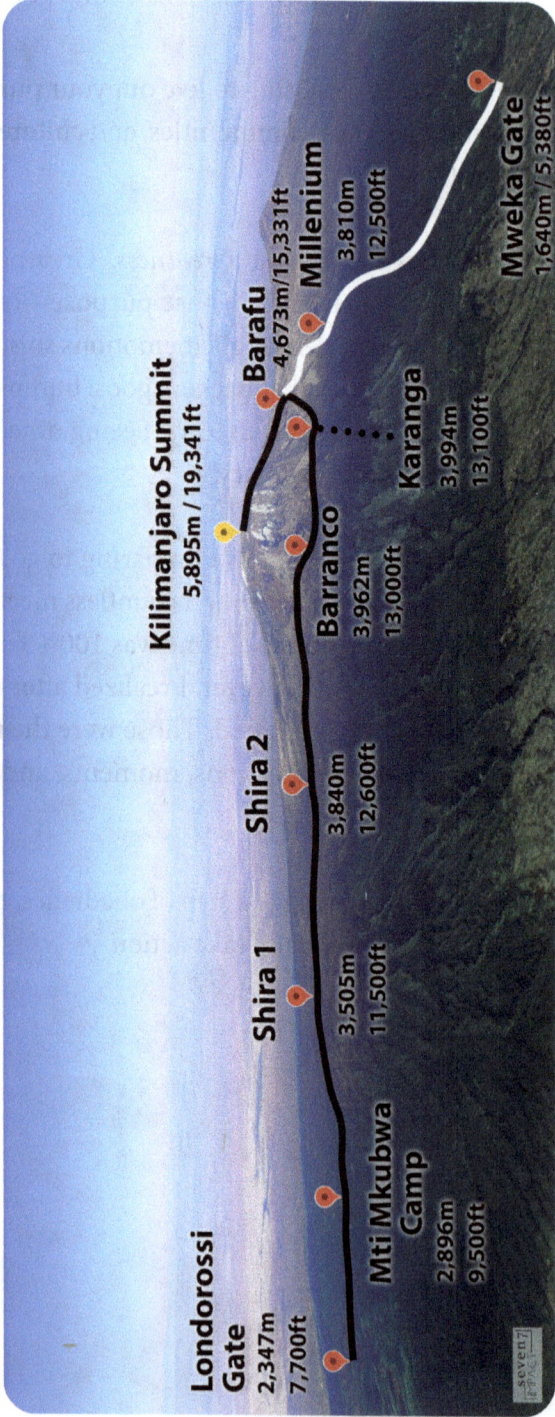

Londorossi Gate
2,347m
7,700ft

Mti Mkubwa Camp
2,896m
9,500ft

Shira 1
3,505m
11,500ft

Shira 2
3,840m
12,600ft

Kilimanjaro Summit
5,895m / 19,341ft

Barranco
3,962m
13,000ft

Karanga
3,994m
13,100ft

Barafu
4,673m/15,331ft

Millenium
3,810m
12,500ft

Mweka Gate
1,640m / 5,380ft

CHAPTER 2

Mt. Elbrus - Die to Yourself

"And if you faithfully obey the voice of the Lord your God, being careful to do all his commandments that I command you today, the Lord your God will set you high above all the nations of the earth..."
Deuteronomy 28:1

On Mt. Elbrus, I was given the word "Death." Not in the sense of physically dying. In this sense, the word means dying to

yourself. Giving up your desires and and intentionally living each day out from who we were designed to be.

I returned from Kilimanjaro with a sense of purpose, operating out of obedience to what I was asked to do. After spending the summer with my family, I immediately headed for the second climb in my 7 Summits Journey—Mt Elbrus. The path to Mt. Elbrus still held many unknowns for me, but I felt excited to visit Russia and explore such a foreign land full of history.

I was on the brink of discovering new people and a new territory. I was ready to see a country full of culture and architecture that is recognized throughout the world. Little did I realize how difficult it would be to release control, nor how different the challenges would be with this leg of my journey.

The Challenge of Preparation

The first challenge in climbing Mt. Elbrus isn't the mountain. It's the bureaucracy. The mountain is in Russia, where getting a visa to enter the country was very challenging, even in 2018. At the time, I was new to this level of international travel. You just don't know what you don't know. There were a lot of hurdles to overcome just so I could climb, such as the application requirements, the paperwork, and the permits required. As with all types of bureaucracy, things don't move quickly.

It's often the little things that threaten a trip like this one. At first, my visa was denied because my passport didn't have enough blank pages left in it. Of all the obstacles–not enough pages! Really? I scrambled to get a new passport quickly before the whole trip was lost. Thankfully, it arrived just in time—two days before I had to leave.

With Elbrus, you're in more of a climber experience versus a hiker experience. You need to wear crampons, use an ice axe, ropes, and more on this climb. You don't learn the movement skills and how to travel on crampons overnight. It takes training your muscles to react to the terrain by instinct through repetition.

Kilimanjaro taught me to value training for a climb and the importance of getting the movement and skills you need. I designed a tailored training regime that included climbs for distance, hikes for altitude training and carrying weight, and strength training at the gym. I was in great condition, but I still had a lot to learn. I would soon find out if I was targeting the right muscle groups. You never know what to expect on the mountain.

Spiritually, I concentrated on being prayerful about scriptures relating to the climb. I still didn't fully understand why my journey was a climbing journey. Why was I called? For whom? I had my purpose and felt I understood it, but what about this journey? I kept thinking about the summit and how I could make it happen. Mentally, I tried to push that back, go into this with open arms, and try not to control the circumstances.

When I arrived in Russia, the first stop was Moscow. One of my favorite ways to take in a new place is by running, so I ran through Red Square. I absorbed the 15th and 16th-century architecture up close, marveling at the decorative towers of the Kremlin. The beautiful red stone of the State Historical Museum was highlighted by white and gold for an impressive display of architectural artistry. The nine colorful topped towers of the Cathedral of St. Basil the Blessed shone like flowers in full bloom above me as I ran.

Interesting Fact: Red Square wasn't named for the red stone on the buildings or for the color red for communism. Red Square was originally named *krasivaya*, which means beautiful in Russian. The Russian word for red, *krasnaya*, is very similar, some claiming they were both the same word in old Russia, so Red Square also translates as "Beautiful Square."

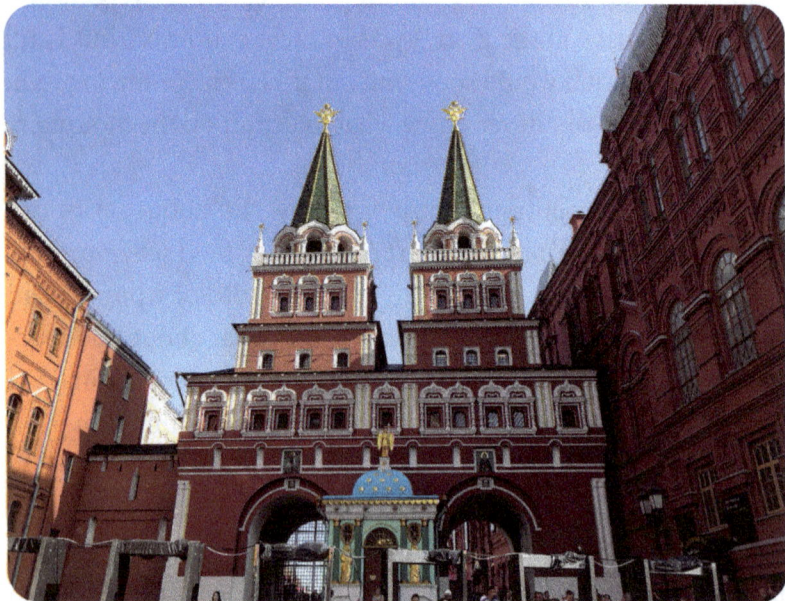

After my run, I felt more relaxed and more open to letting things unfold as He meant them to. Then, I slipped back into attempting to be in control at the airport the next day. I traveled on a budget, and they wanted to charge me so many unplanned fees for my equipment. Tickets and more tickets from one place to another within the airport. It got pretty intense, and I had to keep reminding myself there was nothing I could do about it.

Approaching Elbrus

Same problem, different mountain. How do I even find out how to plan logistics for this climb? There are several Western companies that fly in Western guides and use local people to help. Western guide companies are more expensive and tend to have a less authentic cultural immersion experience.

A little about me…I don't do well bound by a schedule full of touristy stops. I prefer to absorb the local cultures by meeting the people in their communities to fully connect with them. New Reach Foundation is always looking for sustainable legacy projects across the world. We meet the people, strive to understand the local perspectives and identify solutions. We help see these solutions through to execution at a low cost but with a high impact. We get to know the people at a much deeper level.

For Mt Elbrus, I found a Russian company to help me, and with that comes many unknowns. Is the company real? Are they full of corruption? Can I trust them? Will they speak English well enough so we can have basic communication? Will the guide follow safety standards? Will the team equipment be safe and up to date? And more…

What's going to happen? Who are you going to be with?

I connected with a few people at the Mineralnye Vody Airport. Together, we took a 3 1/2-hour bus ride to a mountain hotel in the Baksan Valley near the foothills of Mt. Elbrus (2,100 meters/6,890 feet). I met up with my team here. We spent the next day on a training climb and got to know one another.

Many belonged to a group of Russian guys who were all buddies, being rugged and joyfully giving each other crap. I was an outsider but bonded with a few guys throughout the day and felt more included.

Acclimation and Death

Getting onto Mt Elbrus is interesting. There are two main routes: South and North. We chose the South Route and took the gondolas up to where we started climbing.

We slept in these cold barrels equipped with basic survival needs that held six people. There are electric heaters, but they're not much help against the environment. The toilets are aptly named "House of Pain" and "House of Horror." Here is a photo of the luxury restroom.

We learned how to use our crampons and self-arrest during acclimation climbs. They were really good about teaching us techniques for using ropes, harnesses, and the rest of our gear. The acclimation hikes rewarded us with stunning views throughout the first four days.

I distinctly remember looking out and viewing this mountain range. I found it different from any other range I had seen before. In a different sense of awe, the mountains were stout, wide, big, and absolutely stunning. I basked in these views at every acclimation climb. They were so beautiful and peaceful.

Death is a common word from the start of this climb. Skilled climbers have died on Mt Elbrus. The day before our climb, a couple was killed by lightning on the mountain. There are no trees or rocks. It's just this big open area with huge boulders placed randomly. If you slip or miss a step, you just slide down. Experienced climbers have slid down to their death by hitting a boulder.

It's a pretty quick climb—less than a week—but it's cold. I used crampons and an ice axe for the first time in extreme temperatures, deep snow, and ice. We worked our way up, and I felt very comfortable and fairly strong, thanks to learning about cadence and rhythm on Mt Kilimanjaro. I concentrated on moving slowly and breathing, making sure I practiced good movement skills so they became second nature in this environment.

At one point, we went on a fixed line and clipped in as we got nearer to the summit. This part of the steep, icy slope runs down into a rocky band. If you slide and fall, you're in trouble.

At the last bit to the summit, I realized one thing. No matter how many hours you train or how well you condition yourself, the hard days are going to be hard. This part of the climb was hard. It's a grind. We're feeling the effects of altitude now. Learning how to use crampons is one thing, but traveling in them for hours is something else. We're moving slowly, breathing heavily, and every motion takes more effort.

Through the strain and this physical challenge, I remained confident. I could do this. I'm good. I thought it ironic how many young guys struggled physically and mentally while I moved ahead of them.

A Very Different Summit Experience

I reached the summit with a guy named Kirill, and we spent some time together while waiting for the others. This was Kirill's second attempt at Elbrus. I experienced the challenge of another altitude, worked hard for another summit, and successfully made it to the top. Unlike the blinding weather on Kilimanjaro, this was the first summit where I could truly appreciate the beauty, thanks to the clear sky.

We sat there, catching our breath and taking in the spectacular view with a great sense of accomplishment. I made it to the top of these stout mountains. It was strenuous, but I did it. Suddenly, I realized just how small I was in this world. I was deep in the Caucasus Mountains, just north of the Georgia-Russian border, with little else around. These beautiful mountains look different from anywhere I've been before. It was inspirational.

For me, it became more than a physical achievement. I was traveling further in this journey of what I was asked to do. I was starting to lean into my purpose. I felt confident that I was supposed to be there at that moment. I was on the right path.

The Western summit is the highest point in Europe. The dormant volcano rises 5,642 meters/18,510 feet above sea level. It's the highest stratovolcano in Eurasia and the 10th most prominent peak in the world.

The Eastern summit is 5,621 meters/18,442 feet.

When we got up, the rest of the team reached the top. I looked at the other summit and told the guide, Sergey, "I want to go do that one."

He agreed. "Okay, yeah, cool. You're strong."

One of the Russian guys said, "Yeah, you can go." His friends joined in, wanting to do it too.

Sergey told them, "No, you guys aren't going. You guys aren't strong enough."

These guys were pissed. They had that Russian macho attitude… "We can do it."

Sergey then says, "All right, you want to do it? You've got to prove it to me."

Sergey starts running the guys in this group through tests on the side of the mountain, right off the summit, and he wouldn't let any of them go. Kirill was part of this friend group, and he was going to go down with them. I talked him into climbing the other mountain with me. The three of us—Sergey, Kirill, and I—went up together.

We cut across, descended into a valley, and then worked our way back up. The other guy was struggling, and I remember reaching my point of vulnerability, feeling the strain. The Eastern side was steeper, more dangerous, and technical. Bitter cold settled in, and it grew darker as we climbed. I couldn't help but feel a bit relieved that he was struggling too—this was tough, and knowing I wasn't alone made it easier to keep going.

We were the only three people to attempt to summit the Eastern peak that day. Knowing that we did the extra push and challenge that no one else did was exhilarating. I didn't realize then that the real reward was yet to be discovered on the way down.

We didn't have a view because it was cloudy. Still, as I stood at the monument at the top, it was so rewarding to be at this summit.

The experience was completely different. It was fun. I guess because of the cocky, strong Russian guys talking crap.

Then, we started coming down.

Descent Marked the Word Death

To descend, we went down, worked our way back up, and then went down again in the valley. We came down where the mountains joined. We passed people who were acclimating for the next day, learning how to wear crampons, about rescue situations, and other techniques.

Pausing at the training ground, I looked over my right shoulder and did a full turnaround. Right as that valley came in, what I envisioned was almost animated, with blood coming over and flowing into the bowl of the valley. It's hard to explain. It didn't look like real blood. It was thick, 3D style, and it just flooded everything. It was super clear, and I was taken aback at seeing one of the most beautiful things I've ever seen.

The Western summit was the high point. It was sheer determination that drove me up the Eastern side. I honestly wasn't operating in obedience, but coming down from this summit led to the most pivotal point of the journey for me. I was meant to go to the Eastern Summit. He was in control at all times.

The Cross

As I looked back at the route we had just taken, I remember seeing how it resembled a cross of blood flowing down the center with two cross pieces flowing from side to side. I thought, "Man, that reminds me of the sacrifice of the cross."

I learned later that this route is actually called a cross. It was so vivid, really beautiful to me. I was like, "Holy Cow, right?" When I saw that blood flowing, that was a stamp.

It is Death.

I now had two words on my journey. I had *purpose* and then *death*.

Okay, I hear you.

Jesus stamped the word Death on this climb at that moment. Death is such an important word to the gospel and our daily lives. There are so many possibilities this word can mean. As I continued to follow this journey, the meaning of Death became clearer, but the real revelation came only after I prayed relentlessly for several months about it.

It's not about literally dying. Death is about dying to the self every day. Every day, we need to forget who the world says we are and not get caught up in that nonsense. We must be intentional in knowing who we are and live out that day from our core values, making our decisions based on that. Our daily interactions must be based on our belief system, not the world's.

This was a constant challenge for me during this entire journey to the summits. The temptation to step right back into my career was always there. I didn't want to be half a world apart from my wife and my kids. It would be way more comfortable to be at home, living my old life, doing my job. That old life of mine had to die to make way for this new call. And that's always the way it works. You sacrifice your "yes" to your own worldly desires so that you can say "yes" to God's plan.

Death to self becomes a recentering exercise for Purpose. I've got my Purpose, and now I have a daily practice to refocus on that Purpose.

> Meditation and prayer can be a good thing for us. It's important to guide our hearts, minds, and focus. That morning yoga session clears our mind and prepares us for the day, but if we don't die to our self also, it's limited. It is not about us being clear. It's about us being *aligned* with what we're supposed to do for others.

I can say for certain that if I don't die to myself and refocus my purpose, I will be heavily distracted by many things. When I don't erase all that every single day, my days go very differently.

Stay Calm—I've Got You

After we descended, there was a problem with my flight out, and they wouldn't let me take the bus back. They said I had to get my own vehicle because my flight was moved up an hour earlier, and I would have arrived too late.

So I hired a driver. We got pulled over at a checkpoint along the way. I had no idea what was going to happen. It felt as if the police might pull me out and throw me in a Russian prison. It was intense. Everyone is speaking in Russian, guns drawn and pointed at me!

It's one of those times when you have to remain calm, don't react, and stay on the path. Be who you are and stay in your identity. I also learned another valuable lesson here—to become okay with being uncomfortable. In order to stay calm and see things through, you must also become okay with being uncomfortable.

Things will go wrong. Sometimes, a lot of things will go very wrong, but if you become okay with being uncomfortable, you will be more confident in your true self and in the outcome. Things worked out fine for us. Surprisingly, I didn't have to pay them off to be allowed to continue the trip to the airport. I made it to the airport at the same time as the group who took the bus, and I made my flight out to my next stop in the UAE to assist in labor issues, continuing my work with the non-profit we launched on the previous climb.

New Reach Foundation is a Non-Profit Organization focused on Changing the World through Global Impact.

Our team builds up impoverished local communities through relationships, structure, development, and empowerment for entrepreneurs, leaders, universities, churches, conferences, and representatives. New Reach Foundation strategically arranges companies and organizational partnerships to support startup businesses such as Global Incubators and Global Accelerators.

We are creating a global innovation network with the vision and ambition to transform multi-cultural problems into impactful solutions.

www.newreachfoundation.org

So, What Does This Mean?

The point of the Mt. Elbrus journey is to understand that you've got to get that internal knowing of who you are and let go of the worldly definition of who you are. Then, you can rise to the full fulfillment of what you were created to be.

> Mimetic desire is a concept coined by the French philosopher René Girard, which refers to the tendency of individuals to imitate the desires of others.
>
> According to Girard, human desires are not inherently original but are rather influenced by the desires of others within a social context. This concept suggests that individuals often desire objects, behaviors, or attributes not because of any intrinsic value they possess but because others desire them.
>
> Mimetic desire can lead to competition, rivalry, and conflict as individuals imitate and compete for the same objects of desire. Girard argued that understanding mimetic desire is crucial for understanding human behavior, social dynamics, and the roots of violence and conflict in society.

Too often, we live our lives through the lens of what others want or do. We're "keeping up with the Joneses." Sometimes, we do it out of envy, and other times, we do it to model success. Part of the meaning of the word death in this context is to let those external aiming points die.

We make better daily decisions when we know who we are and live according to our own defined identity versus the world's. Strive to be open to what will happen and what will come from your actions as you interact with the world. It can be uncomfortable at first, and that is a good discomfort. It allows us to become who we are meant to be.

We are valuable. There are so many people out there who don't know who they are and know their self-worth back to their purpose. **It becomes impactful when we're striding in that greatness and know our self-worth.**

Are you ready to let go of what the world thinks you should be and embrace your true self?

So now, I had Purpose and Death from Him to guide me. On to the third summit—Kosciuszko.

Western Summit
6,190m
20,310ft

Eastern Summit
5,933m
19,470ft

Barrels (Camp)
4,267m
14,000ft

Start of Climb
2,195m
7,200ft

seven7
IMPACT

CHAPTER 3

Kosciuszko - Remain Obedient

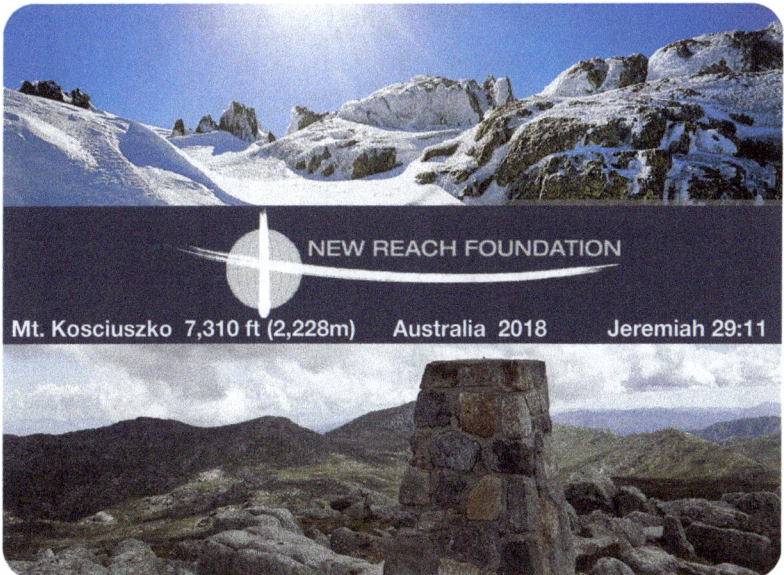

*"For I know the plans I have for you, says the Lord. They
are plans for good and not for evil, to give you
a future and a hope."*
Jeremiah 29:11

Obedience is hearing your instructions and then taking action without always seeing the end result of those actions. When doubt creeps in and obstacles get in your way, faith gives you the courage to follow through with what you have been asked to do.

Within the mountain climbing world, there is an ongoing debate about the location of my next summit. Some believe the 7 Summits should be the highest mountain on a continental mass. Others believe it should be the highest mountain on a continental mass and its surrounding islands.

Kosciusko is part of the original 7 Summits list compiled by Richard Bass and is the tallest mountain on the Australian mainland at 2,228 meters/7,310 feet. New Guinea's Carstensz Pyramid (Puncak Jaya) is higher at 4,884 meters/16,024 feet, and future climbers thought it should be the 7 summit mountain. Some climbers choose to do both in their 7 summit quests.

I had planned to climb both summits, but political unrest at the time canceled my climb to the Carstensz Pyramid. My next climb in the 7 Summits journey became limited to Kosciuszko.

A Father's Day Message

For many of my climbs, their impact began before we reached the mountain. On Father's Day of 2018, I was camping with my family in the US. We were at a campsite we often stay at, so we are very familiar with what's normal there. That night, I dreamed the most vivid dream.

I was just coming out of my career to answer the call and take those four steps I believe God put before me—1) leave my job; 2) climb the 7 Summits; 3) start a non-profit; 4) fund it myself. I traveled extensively in my previous roles, so being called to travel did not concern me. Often, the challenge is understanding what His messages actually mean.

I fell asleep during our campout and entered a dream where this happened: I walked into this prestigious airline status club with men in suits. A guy wearing a black suit, shirt, and tie walked up to me and said, "Go to Tandora."

I woke up. "What's Tandora?"

Immediately, I pulled out my phone and Googled Tandora. Tandora is a place in Queensland, Australia. Pictures of a farming community of cattle herders filled my screen.

How strange. I wondered what the dream meant.

Then, I looked out the RV window and saw hundreds—perhaps thousands—of cattle surrounding us. This has never happened before at this spot and has never happened since.

"Wow. Conviction. I hear you," I said to the Lord.

Obedience is the natural next step on the seven pillars of this journey. As I reflect on the full story of Kosciuszko, I realize that being obedient creates a huge impact on our lives. It's not a coincidence this happened on Father's Day. He gave me a clear message of what I was to do.

Jeremiah 29:11 became the inspired scripture for this trip. Throughout my preparation, I struggled and prayed for this trip in my home office. He kept guiding me back to Jeremiah 29:11.

"For I know the plans I have for you, declares the Lord,
plans for welfare and not for evil,
to give you a future and a hope."
Jeremiah 29:11 (ESV)

I kept thinking, "This isn't it." This scripture is overused—it cannot be the one for Kosciuszko. After several months of prayer, God continued to place Jeremiah 29:11 on this mountain. I finally gave in and said, "Okay, Lord. I get it. It's that simple. That's what it is."

Listening before setting out on your journey is important. Proper preparation also sets things in motion for the people we encounter. God's word leads us through the good and bad moments ahead. When we focus and tune in to His message, it keeps us moving forward.

Never Assume You Know Everything

I try to plan all my climbs according to the local seasons. I soon discovered that I didn't get Kosciuszko's seasons right.

After a grueling 16-hour flight from Vancouver, Canada, to Sydney, Australia, I met up with Melanie. She had a work event, and having someone with me gave me a mental boost. We drove six hours to Thredbo, where the prep work started.

I live at a higher altitude than Kosciuszko and expected a quick climb to the summit. I decided to skip looking for a guide and company to help me with this mountain. "I'm just going to do this and knock this out," I told Melanie. We would only be here one day. I planned on getting up early and ticking this climb off my summit list. Then, we would turn around and head to Sydney for Melanie's work event.

Through light research, I discovered that you could climb Kosciuszko any time of the year. I didn't even question it. It was October, but I didn't realize it was also the start of the mud season for them and that everything would be closed. Not until I got there, and by then, it was too late to turn back.

Kosciuszko is a ski resort in a national park about 6 hours west of Sydney. People visit to mountain bike, ski, and snowboard. All the snow was melting off at that time, creating a colossal mess. It became too muddy for snowboarding or mountain biking. There wasn't enough snow for any other snow sports. October was the worst time to do anything in the mountains.

The resort was deserted when I got there. I asked questions about what it's like on the mountain at the shops. I always received, "Nobody's up there now" as a response. I figured I better get this summit done. Good thing it's only 2,228 meters/7,310 feet.

A Simple Hike. Easy, Right?

Since I didn't have a guide, I loaded GPS points onto my Gaia GPS. That proved to be the smartest move I made for this climb. At least I had a trail to follow.

As I started hiking up the mountain, the weather became terrible. Strong 80-90 kilometer winds ripped through me. The snow deepened, and the temperature plummeted. I soon found myself trudging through a whiteout condition.

If you've never climbed a mountain in a total whiteout, it's very disorienting. It's possible to fall over while standing still because your body thinks you're still moving. You can't navigate the terrain by contouring the landscape.

Thankfully, I had those GPX points to guide me. I couldn't see any markers to tell me where the trail led. Even with my app guiding me, self-defeating thoughts still crept into my mind. I kept thinking, "I'm turning around. I'm not doing this."

Pushing Through To The Summit

I was lucky. Devices are susceptible to cold conditions, and I could have lost my GPS points. I tried not to think about that as I pushed through the self-defeating thoughts and beelined for the summit.

That summit climb became one of the most miserable journeys for me. Our paths are often filled with obstacles along the way, and I learned one thing about myself during this trip. Fighting my way through the force of nature on my own did not give me the same satisfaction as making the summit with teammates by my side.

This summit also taught me two lessons: you should never be negligent in your preparation, and obedience will see you through your negativity.

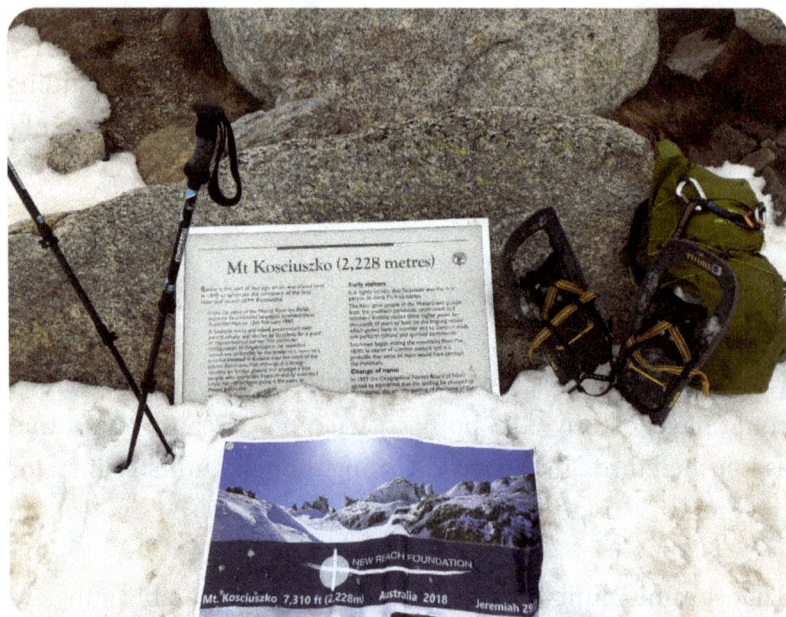

I failed in a comprehensive preparation process for this climb. I assumed Kosciuszko was an easy climb and stopped at light research. I did not try to understand the weather conditions or seasons completely. I only packed a couple of light layers, and I did not fully equip myself for a whiteout condition.

A little struggle through rough weather on my own allowed negative self-talk to enter my mind. We are all guilty of this. We allow negativity to enter our lives, even in easy situations—or when we discover something isn't as easy as expected.

Obedience led me through the difficulty I encountered on this climb. I leaned on my faith and pushed through the weather and negative self-talk.

The word *obedience* was not marked in that hike or climb. It was marked in the trip, and a precursor to obedience is faith. It's important to understand faith before you can understand what being obedient means.

> Faith means belief, firm persuasion, assurance, conviction, and faithfulness. Faith is confidence in what we hope for and the assurance that the Lord is working even though we cannot see it. Faith knows that no matter the situation in our lives or someone else's, the Lord is working on it.

You need that undeniable conviction and faith to see you forward through the unknowns, the fears, and the self-doubts that creep in on your journey.

Don't Give in to the Negative Self Talk

We had a good plan. Melanie and I would go to Sydney, and I would fly to Tandora. My uncertainty almost ruined that plan.

Flying to Tandora would add a lot of expense to our trip. Maybe I was wrong and He was just telling me to come to Australia. I brought all this to Melanie, and she helped me see that cutting corners now on what He asked me to do wasn't right. I needed to go to Tandora.

Melanie had time to spare before she had to speak at the conference, and we were alone while our children were on the other side of the world. We decided to explore Sydney together. Even during our downtime, we had impactful moments with strangers.

There was one moment when we walked by a man with dirty clothes and sad eyes. God put this man onto my heart, so we stopped to talk to him. I gave him my necklace with Jeremiah 29:11 on it, thinking, "Maybe he's the reason I was supposed to be on this trip."

I was justifying not going to Tandora because I did not want to spend the money, time, energy, and everything needed to make the trip. I kept falling back on the thought, "Oh, He was just pointing me to go to Australia."

But then I remembered Jeremiah 29:11 and how our journeys are about other people as much as ourselves. I had to make sure I did this right. Until I knew differently, my journey was not complete. I pushed back my doubts and got on that flight.

On the plane, I had an amazing conversation with a family sitting next to me. They thanked me for showing up for them and giving them what they needed to hear. I thought maybe this was why God needed me here. Perhaps the dream was about connecting with these people and giving them the strength for something I cannot see. I just didn't know.

When I landed, I learned that Tandora is in the bush. Tandora is a rural community with a population of approximately a dozen people. It seemed strange that this could be where God meant for me to travel, so my reaction was to try to take control again.

I reached out to a few churches, asking if anything was happening in this area right now. No one gave me any useful information, so I kept driving deeper into the bush. Eventually, I reached a property marked with a sign that said, "No Guns Allowed." I took that as a good sign that I wouldn't be shot at and drove up the dirt drive.

Stop Having to Justify Things to Others

His call for me to visit Tandora came five months before this, in June, on that Father's Day campout. Countless meetings led up to this point, and I met with so much adversity from my peers. They thought I was crazy for following a dream that I believed came from God.

I could not shake off that dream despite the objections from my peers. It wasn't just a dream. It was a message. While I felt confident in Him, I failed to have conviction. I felt lonely—like an outcast.

Instead of praying for guidance in my obedience, I prayed for results others would recognize. I followed God's direction, praying, "Lord, give me something tangible I can show them for this journey."

I continued to look for justification for why I was being obedient. I could not release control of the outcome, nor could I accept the possibility of not being able to see the outcome. Not yet. I wasn't ready to release control and be confident in my obedience.

That was my mindset as I pulled up to a little house. A couple of people sat on a patio. A man with a close-cropped beard and a weathered hat approached me. He pointed his finger at my face and said, "I know who you are."

That was a shocking moment. How could he know me? I thought he meant, "Get out of here. You're not welcome." Turns out that news travels fast in small communities in Tanzania, as it does in the Midwestern United States. As he invited me to a tour of the area in his truck, I soon realized I was very welcome to his home.

His name was Lindsay, AKA Butch. I was honored to share the gospel with him and his two companions. It broke down the barriers, and he took me out to show me his land. I got to know his grandkids, who showed me their favorite places and gave me some fossils from the land.

Lindsay shared with me so many stories of the land, the mangroves, everything. He's not a believer. None of them are believers. I don't think they had heard about Jesus before I arrived, but they seemed to love hearing about the gospel.

I spent a day with them in a beautifully diverse landscape full of kangaroos, Tasmanian devils, and incredible birdlife. Lindsay kept sharing some of the best stories I've heard in a long time. His grandkids talked about koalas and how people from the University of San Diego came to study them.

Nothing crazy happened. That tangible story I was looking for did not happen. It was purely a day of pouring into each other, loving on them. I made memories with new friends that I'll treasure for a lifetime.

I left there feeling sad—maybe a little discouraged. It took a toll on me—emotionally and spiritually. Things weren't complete. I still didn't have that cool story that others expected me to return with to prove my conviction.

The next day was my birthday, and I planned on spending it working out and running through the streets of Sydney. A friend encouraged me to go to Manly Beach. Usually, I would say no to anything touristy, but Melanie was busy, and I had some time.

I took a ferry and put on headphones. I tuned everyone around me out while I became absorbed in worship music and focused on God. I felt Him highlighting a girl, which made me hesitant. I shouldn't be noticing her.

But He insisted on placing her on my heart, so I started talking to her. We got off the boat and had lunch together. I felt the Lord saying, "Jeremiah 29:11 is for her," while she told me about herself.

I said, "You know, this is going to sound a little weird. I really feel Jesus is putting the verse Jeremiah 29:11 on my heart for you."

She went into total breakdown with a shell-shocked look on her face. "You're an angel. God delivered you to me."

She was going through a divorce, and things were rough. In her turmoil, she turned to the Bible and kept reading Jeremiah 29:11 over and over again. She was rooted in that verse—out of 31,102 verses in the Bible. That's the one she's in and only in.

He sent me to give her faith and confidence in Him. It was positioned in a way that I was just a vessel. I fought that verse so much, and it led to changing this woman's entire walk. It gave her the confidence to get through the divorce. She's now remarried and has a life that's aligned with the Kingdom.

> Sometimes, you're going to be in the heart of your journey where it doesn't seem like anything is happening. You just have to keep moving forward, finding encouragement from new places until you get to the end, and have faith, even if you don't get to see the final outcome of your actions.

I look at all the events that led up to our conversation, and I love everything about it. That pivotal moment in her life happened because I leaned into my faith and followed Him out of *obedience*. This word came to me out of prayer time, and it was stamped throughout the whole trip.

I believe He gave me this experience out of my obedience. I feel as if it was a birthday gift to me. "Son, I'm well pleased. Here's a gift. You wanted to see something, here's something. You went to Tandora. You did everything I asked of you."

When we have that conviction and don't question it, we're in a relationship. We can then hear something. We can be wrong with what we hear. Maybe the Tandora dream was bogus. Whatever—it doesn't matter. It's that conviction and the heart behind it. Even though we will likely make mistakes along the way, above all else, He knows our hearts.

When we take action in obedience because of faithfulness, whether it's right or wrong, it doesn't matter. He knows our hearts and counts what is in our hearts, not merely the results of our actions. It is so beautiful, and it's so amazing.

God put this woman in front of me who needed something so badly and allowed me to help her. He gives us these gifts and blessings not because He has to but because He wants to. And it's encouraging.

When you're striding in that relationship with Him, He will bless you. I can't tell you how. I don't know how, but He will. It goes back to the greatness and the purpose. It's all connected.

To see somebody's world change is tangible, and that's amazing. I connected her with a local church where she lives, and she became active in the church. That's Kingdom impact. I was blessed to witness how my *obedience* changed this woman's life. We don't always get to see that.

So, What Does This Mean?

The Kosciuszko climb was a God-filled journey for me. Maybe you're a person rooted in the gospel, maybe not.

Obedience is the word that marks Kosciuszko, and it is supported by *faith*. Everyone is putting their faith into something. What are you putting your faith into?

Understanding your faith will help you understand *obedience*. It will help you be obedient and lead you where you need to go. Faith will give you the confidence to be obedient and follow through with the right actions. *Obedience* is not deserving of immediate or any known outcome. For *obedience* to work at full potential, you need to release any need for immediate acknowledgment or justification.

So far, in this journey, I discovered my purpose and how I can realign with my core values on a daily basis. Now, I choose to live in *obedience* and have faith that He knows my path. I'm doing the right thing without the need to control or see the outcome.

The beautiful thing about this lesson is that we don't even have to be right. We have to be committed. I could have been mistaken about the call to Tanadora. Maybe I didn't understand what it meant 100%. That's okay. The important thing is that I took that step into the unknown of what I could not see. I had faith that staying on my path would make something unforeseen happen.

The true power is in the release. Instead of trying to control what's happening, let go and be obedient. It's tough to do this in life and business because it's human nature to be self-sufficient. The world teaches us to trust in ourselves, but before we can truly create an impact, we often need to let go and trust in something we cannot see.

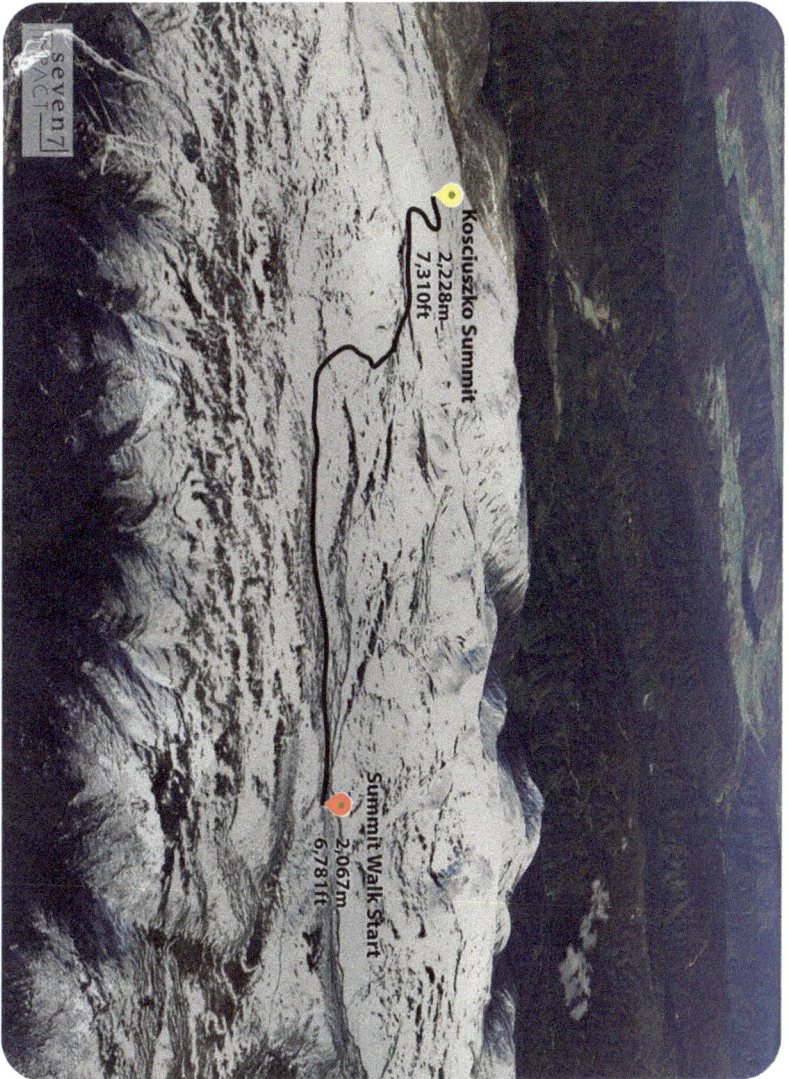

Kosciuszko Summit
2,228m
7,310ft

Summit Walk Start
2,067m
6,781ft

CHAPTER 4

Aconcagua - Rest in Confidence

"I have said these things to you,
that in me you may have peace.
In the world you will have tribulation. But take heart;
I have overcome the world."
John 16:33

Rest is confidence in who you are in your belief system. When you trust in that relationship, you limit the what-if moments that can hold you back.

For the next step in the 7 Summits journey, God took me to Argentina. Aconcagua is a mountain that people dream of climbing and devote their lives to training for. It's the highest mountain in South America at 6,961 meters / 22,838 feet and the tallest outside of Asia.

The South American culture and people are incredible. I fell in love with how close their families are, their outlook on life, and their resiliency. The Argentine culture added vibrancy to my trip through its unique blend of European and Latin American influences mixed in with their indigenous traditions.

Self-Doubt

Aconcagua was the fourth summit in one year. I felt good as I pursued this journey. I had been given three words, *Purpose*, *Death*, and *Obedience*, during my first three climbs. Everything was lining up, making a little more sense, and starting to really come together.

I had a lot more to consider with the Aconcagua climb. The weather is volatile, and you never know what you will encounter. You better have your gear and technical requirements in place for this one. It's high altitude, just under 23,000 feet, and a 17-day expedition. The level of difficulty just jumped from a 7 out of 10 to a 15 out of 10.

Aconcagua has a lower success rate than other mountains within the 7 Summits, but I was confident I could handle it by this time. I knew how to plan for the unexpected better. I was more physically prepared because I had been training. I succeeded with the other climbs, which gave me confidence, and I was getting this international travel thing down, which makes the entire process a bit more comfortable.

Despite the experience I gained on the earlier climbs, I started Aconcagua with a significant mistake. I arrived late...very late...the day before the climb. The next day, I scrambled to get permits, met with others, and arranged guidance from a local guide company.

Self-Doubt Creeps In

I won't lie. I was nervous about it. Even though I went through the prep work and felt confident about learning the tricks of the trade, I just didn't know my abilities or what I was capable of on a mountain like Aconcagua. To make things worse, from the start of this climb, I was struggling with GI issues.

Can I do this? Am I good enough to do this? It's a big climb—a big step in my journey.

Awe-Struck by the Andes

Before we started hiking, everyone had smiles on their faces and was laughing. This is the beginning, the most optimistic moment of the climb.

It is hard to describe the sheer beauty of the Andes Mountains. It's breathtakingly beautiful, vast, and awe-inspiring. When I think of the word "awesome," this is what they must have had in mind.

We could feel the history of this place and the Incan culture just by looking at the mountains. This was the moment when we checked in with ourselves and did some risk management.

> It's amazing how the Inca civilization rose sometime in the 13th century and adapted to the challenging terrain of the Andes Mountains. Their technology and architecture were quite advanced in using terracing methods, creating stable roads, and building structures that could withstand land disruptions. You can still find evidence of their irrigation systems, palaces, temples, and structures all throughout the Andes.

It's best to deal with self-management and face these things before you need them. This is where I fell back on what I learned from my mission trips. I took on the leadership role and checked in with everyone. I watched my teammates, reviewed the plan and the agenda, and built those bonds with people that would last long after my 7 Summit journey.

My GI issues worsened for the first few days, and I felt less optimistic about this climb. By the third day into the ascent, I felt better. Interacting and making friends with a couple of other climbers boosted my confidence. I helped relieve some of their anxiety about the climb by sharing the knowledge I had gained from the previous summits. It opened my eyes to the fact that I had something to offer my teammates on this climb. I could help them have a better experience.

Maybe I Wasn't So Wise...

At one point, we had to make a glacial river crossing of the Vacas River. Some people take mules across it, while others walk through it. I had a bright idea that I would not experience this climb right if I didn't walk through it.

Two of us chose to walk across the river. We took off our boots and socks and rolled up our pants. The water, which had come from melting snow high in the mountains, was so cold it hurt.

Our legs were instantly numb. Then, that deep-seated pain hit. I'm talking about real pain that hurts like nothing I've felt before. Getting my boots back on once I hit the other side was challenging, to say the least.

We slowly gained altitude up the Vacas Valley, heading north, during which I spent the first 15 minutes stomping my feet to get the feeling back in my legs. I was certain I wouldn't make the same decision next time. Still, I'm thankful I didn't take the mules that day. It was an awesome kinesthetic learning experience.

Aconcagua Base Camp

The Vacas Valley is one of the most absolutely beautiful places on the planet. Copper glints off the mountains, and life-supporting waterways run through it. The climb to the base camp leading from the river is one of the most inspiring hikes I've been on.

The Plaza Argentina base camp at 4,200 meters/13,780 feet was more equipped than many camps. We slept in tents that were more like bunkhouses. We ate real meals in a designated dining room tent. It was New Year's Eve, and we had a real bash there.

Team building spirits were high, even as some people were sick and exhausted from the altitude and exertion. People were starting to break down a little, yet they were determined. Myself included. I started to have GI issues again, and then bronchitis-like symptoms settled in. Luckily, a climbing mate shared her flu packets with me, and in two days, I was much better.

We did our acclimation climbs at the base camp. We climbed up a way to get used to the elevation and then came back down to rest. This is the point where we were just starting to get to the snow line.

Sometimes, this phase can be stressful, and this is where you really have to pull together as a team to get through it. This time, our guide allowed the stress to get to him momentarily, and he started lashing out at the team. Our team dynamics kicked in, and we pulled together to not let this setback sink the ship.

We navigated our way through huge ice columns called Penitentes to get to Camp One during our second acclimation climb. Maintaining our balance while maneuvering through them was a very unique experience. It felt more natural when we trekked through them again when we continued up the mountain.

Penitentes are large inverted icicles that grow out of the ground and are formed by wind blowing and freezing water particles together. They get their name because they resemble rows of people kneeling in repentance.

One of the most rewarding things about climbing Aconcagua via the Polish Glacier Traverse Route is the 360-degree experience you get from the expedition. You're on the eastern face up to the Plaza Argentina Base Camp. You ascend the northern face to the high camps. Then, on the descent, you traverse the western face, exiting the park on the southern face.

We had no porters on this trip. Our packs weighed over 50 pounds and felt much heavier at this altitude. The weather became colder as we ascended, pushing through a persistent wind. It was "breathe, step, breathe, step." Patience and listening to our bodies for signs of altitude sickness were vital to getting through this climb.

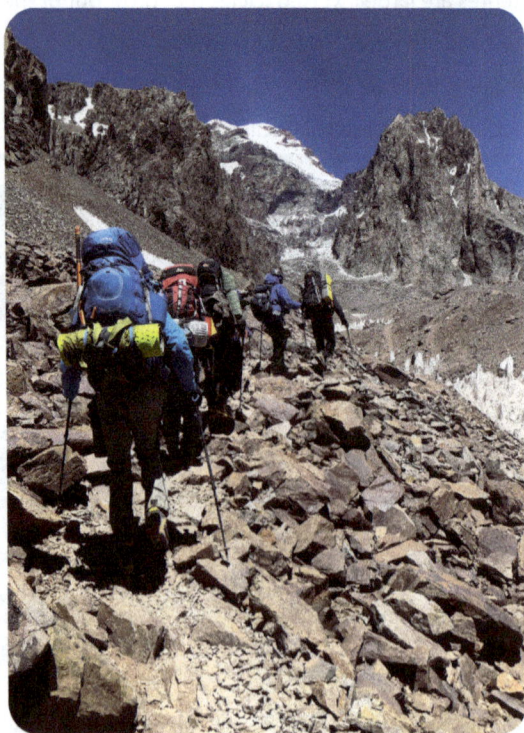

Reaching Camp Two at 5,500 meters/18,044 feet was a celebration in itself, but that's not all. This camp overlooked the valley and the Andes Mountains. They claim this mountain has a soul, and I could believe it as I felt the breathtaking view lift my spirits. It was the most beautiful thing I've ever seen.

Then Everything Changed

We had a solid plan for this climb. We would stay at Camp Two and then move on to Camp Three and the Summit Push. Everything seemed perfectly set until the weather changed. It came in hard and fast.

Our guide assured us. "I've never been in Camp Two longer than two days. Don't worry. It's fine."

The weather rolled in, flattened tents, and iced everything over. Violent winds ripped through the remaining tents. The temperature dropped dramatically, freezing our world in absolute misery where it was impossible to get even slightly warm.

I hate tents and don't sleep well in them, but that was the least of my worries. My air mattress had a catastrophic failure and wouldn't hold air. There was no patching it because we could not find a leak anywhere.

That air mattress was crucial to surviving this storm. We have our foam mat layer, and then, on top of that, the air mattress insulates us from the freezing ground. Without it, I was in real danger of hypothermia. I became even more sleep-deprived than normal, and hypothermia set in. I kept shivering and shaking uncontrollably while the tent I shared with two other guys pitched violently back and forth in the icy wind.

Ice dripped off the tent. The temperature plummeted below any level I've been in before. I wore more layers, but it didn't provide much barrier against such a force of nature. The flapping of the tent reverberated through my head constantly, and the winds wailed. Nature was not giving me any respite to find a moment's peace so I could regain some of my sanity.

Oddly, I chose this time to read the book *Minus 148 Degrees: The First Winter Ascent of Mount McKinley*, which tells the story of those who died there. It made me feel better, surprisingly. Reading the extenuating circumstances brought a sense of, I don't know, camaraderie to what I was experiencing at the time.

A tent flattened by high winds.

Just Let It Out

All we could do was lay there and wait out the weather. I froze, shivered, and watched the tent whip back and forth. Icicles formed, and I battled with God as nature unleashed its power onto our small camp.

It was one of the biggest battles I've had with Him in my life. "Why am I here? Why did you do this? I don't like this. I'm not a climber."

I vented all my frustrations, some of which didn't even make sense. "You're crazy! I'm doing this for you. This sucks!" I kept going through a bunch of absurd objections that I can't even remember now.

He patiently and calmly listened to me vent. Then, everything went still. The wind suddenly stopped and the deafening noise pounding my head died down, allowing His words through. "Scott, I didn't ask you to summit these mountains. I asked you to climb them."

I received my answer, loud and clear, during that moment of silence before the howling winds kicked up again. That was all it took for clarity to settle in and allow me to let go. He stamped the word *rest* on me.

I Didn't Ask You to Summit

At that moment, I realized I was allowing the enemy to drive a wedge between me and the greatness I would gain from my obedience. I was wrestling with Him, with the idea that "I have to get to the summit." I should have rested in faith that He knew the way and the destination.

Our lead guide had turned from happy-go-lucky to pessimistic. All my climbing mates were negative, and I was playing the perpetual optimist, commanding, "It will happen. We will summit."

It was so miserable.

Until He stamped that word *rest* on me. It took 100% of Scott's control out of the situation and made it all right again. One hundred percent of the weight suffocating me and pressuring me was lifted away. When we truly rest—and find that internal sense of peace—that's when things come alive.

We were trapped at Camp Two for five days. We ran out of food, but thankfully, a porter brought us up more. We lost the extra days we scheduled into our trip's plan. We needed to make careful decisions from here on out. Some people had pre-scheduled flights to make and time-sensitive permits.

Beyond 16 Strong Russians

I look up to Russian climbers. They were on all these mountains I climbed, and they are often the strongest climbers. In my experience, they're usually the toughest, grittiest, and most determined. On the way up to Camp Colera at 5,970 meters/19,000 feet, we met 16 Russian climbers who were on their way down without making the summit.

If they couldn't summit, what were our chances? The fact that they gave up worried us, and we had to have a team meeting upon reaching the camp.

The team decided to move forward in the morning, but we lost a valued member. She was athletic and strong, but she mentally shut down. It was her third attempt, and she decided not to participate in our team summit push.

We had a knowledgeable and insightful guide to help us reach the summit. He's a world-renowned Argentine climber and the first Argentine to complete the 7 Summits. He was instinctively dialed into the mountain, and his timetable was dialed in. He knew when it was time to move and how to operate a good climb on Aconcagua. We followed him, passing other groups on our way up.

During a tough stretch, two of our guys weren't going to make it. Our guide wanted to send one or both of them down. They struggled to move safely as a team. My sense of team dynamics kicked in and we didn't send them down. I stepped in to assist our leader and kept the team together, making it possible to support both of them.

Our destination was Canaleta Cave at 22,000 feet, and this segment became the slowest hike of my life. At that altitude, you're moving slowly with incredible effort. We covered very little distance at a time—it was miserable and so very slow. It seemed as if we would never reach the cave.

We finally made it to the cave and rested. We kept thinking, "Holy Cow! That was a lot of work. Do we want to continue this climb?"

Yes, We Do!

We decided to continue towards the summit. For our guide, it was well over the thirtieth time for him, but no less of an accomplishment. He bowed, submitted, and gave a speech in Spanish through tears at the summit. Witnessing his love for the mountain and the community was a very impactful moment for me.

It was the highest I had ever been, and I was pretty emotional about it, too. I even pulled out my go-pro and asked a guy to record me as I poured out my emotions at making the climb. Sadly, I don't have that video. He thought it was running when it wasn't.

We stayed up on the beautiful summit and rested for an hour, basking in our accomplishment and sharing a sense of achievement with the next team that summited afterward. I reflected on the sense of peace God gave me during that pivotal moment in the middle of the storm while looking over the splendor in front of us. I marveled at how God brought me to a place where I could achieve something I never expected to do before. I felt honored that He was allowing me to use this experience in a way that allowed others to achieve their summit when they may have otherwise given up.

A Hard Descent

The descent was the hardest part of Aconcagua. I was physically exhausted after focusing on the summit for so long. My knees and body hurt. People say it's half over, but it was less than half over for me.

Going down was challenging. Statistically, more people die on the way down these mountains than on the way up. Some of us moved quickly, while some were slower. We were not in unison as a team. We were all over the place.

Climbing Aconcagua was an eye-opener for me, showing me what climbing a serious mountain means. It was quite incredible and something I never dreamed of doing. I'll never regret following His call.

The word *rest* has so much meaning. I had to really stretch myself to endure these conditions. This journey was preparing me to be able to handle any challenges that may come in my life—those challenges in the midst of a battle.

Rest in Him. "I told you to climb, not to summit." Words matter.

So, What Does This Mean?

In the Seven Summits journey, we have the following prayerful words so far:

- On Kilimanjaro, he gave the word *purpose*. We should meet people where they are at while on our path to greatness.

- On Mt. Elbrus, He gave the word *death* to show how I need to let go of how the world defines me before I can know and understand who I really am.
- On Kosciusko, He gave the word *obedience*. We are called to obediently follow, even when we don't understand–just follow, be obedient.

And now, on Aconcagua, He gave the word *rest*. We are to *rest* in what we believe. This was the pivotal point for me. God took my life from the midst of chaos on the mountain, literally, to calm in that instant. My circumstances on the mountain were still terrible, but I was able to *rest* in Him despite the external circumstances.

Rest determines how we respond to what's in front of us. It is how we carry ourselves forward in confidence. Rest allows us to proceed in alignment with Him. These first four words are critical to helping us discover how much more we're capable of achieving.

> In our day-to-day lives, the tendency is to push, push, push to reach that next milestone. We struggle and strive.
>
> Rest is not leisure.
>
> Rest is a confidence. A knowing. Confidence that you are enough. That He is sufficient for you. You rest confidently in that knowing. It is a spiritual rest, separate and apart from the physical rest we often seek.

Throughout this journey, I've also discovered one critical piece of understanding how this works. It doesn't matter what's going on around us. It doesn't matter if the wind's howling, if the very storm around us threatens to whisk us away, or how the thunderous claps of the tents are pounding into our ears. The power of *rest* is internal.

The change in *rest* came from within me. It's that internal change that will allow us to respond to the external circumstances we cannot control. Rest helps you filter out all the noises that distract you from your conviction.

With rest, you become confident in who you are. When you trust in your team, leaders, or the tools you use to get through your day, you don't live according to the "what ifs." Without the what-ifs distracting you, you're striding in the right direction, and your focus is where it should be.

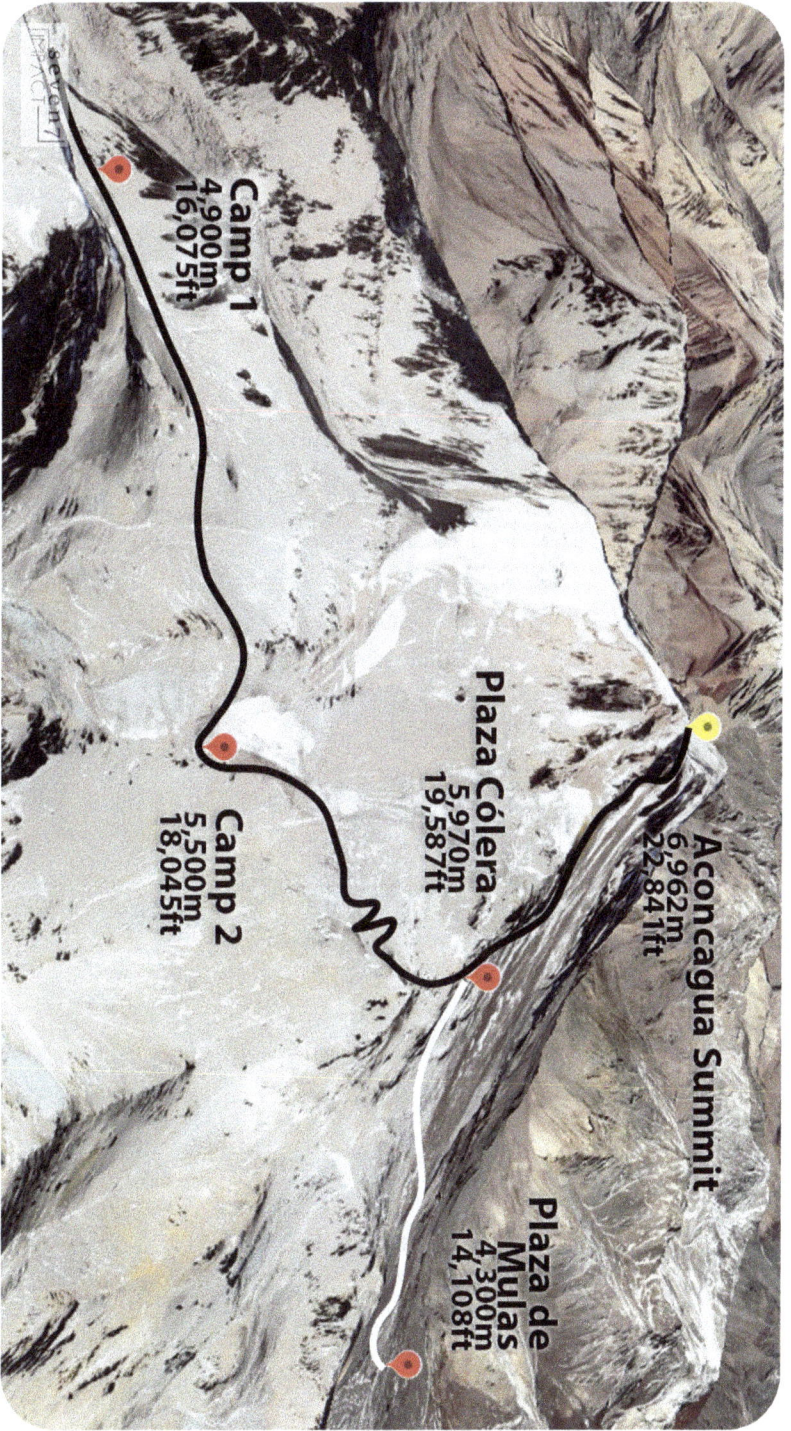

Camp 1
4,900m
16,075ft

Camp 2
5,500m
18,045ft

Plaza Cólera
5,970m
19,587ft

Aconcagua Summit
6,962m
22,841ft

Plaza de
Mulas
4,300m
14,108ft

CHAPTER 5

Denali -It's All About Relationship

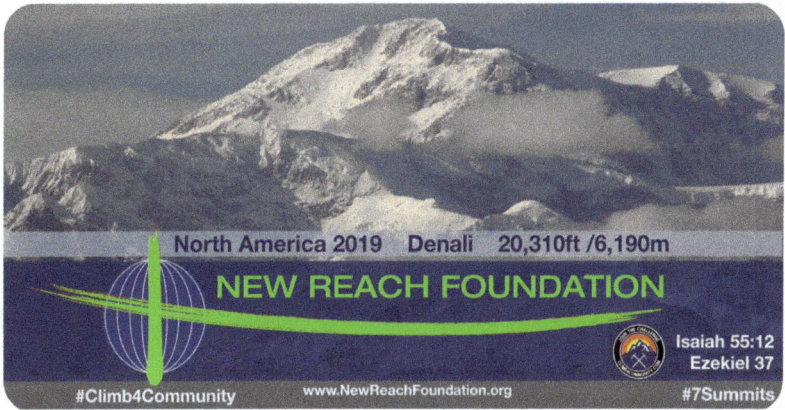

North America 2019   Denali   20,310ft /6,190m
NEW REACH FOUNDATION
Isaiah 55:12
Ezekiel 37
#Climb4Community   www.NewReachFoundation.org   #7Summits

"For you shall go out in joy and be led forth in peace; the mountains and the hills before you shall break forth into singing, and all the trees of the field shall clap their hands."
Isaiah 55:12

Relationship is knowing there's no way I can do this in my own strength and surrendering fully to that fact. This opens the bridge of opportunity to start connecting and sharing with others for even more success and personal fulfillment.

On to Denali in south-central Alaska. With a summit elevation of 6,190 meters/20,310 feet, it's the highest mountain in
North America.

Denali can be intimidating. The mountain is a serious climb
across glaciers. You will meet up with very hard ice on the upper
mountain and 50-degree steepness. Right from the start, you're
dealing with ice—it's super hard, dangerous, and beautiful.

I had more to prepare for with this climb, both physically and
mentally. I needed to learn new movement skills for the difference in terrain. We will be on crampons throughout the climb,
and every climber has to be able to stay in rhythm with the team
or risk death. We climb with a heavy pack and pull a sled loaded
with gear and supplies. Denali is a very controlled climb, requir-
ing everyone to be in shape and ready for this one before they
allow people on the mountain.

Did I question my ability to do this one? I felt good about it and
excited, but I had my moments of doubt. How do I train for pulling a sled on this terrain? How do I climb with it, and how well
can I maneuver the sled on the climb?

Just Do It

Many recommend climbing Mt Rainier as preparation for Denali.
I didn't do that. I just jumped right from Aconcagua to Denali.
Denali is known as the most difficult one of the 7 Summits, so I
was calculated in my approach to training with this one.

We carry between 60 and 70 pounds in our packs and pull up to 80 pounds on a sled. I have to be able to manage this while wearing snowshoes on the approach. There are a lot of skills to master and gear to handle on this climb. There's also a real danger of falling into a crevasse on the glaciers.

Frankly, I was intimidated by this one. Even though I did four summits before it and had over a year's experience to prepare me for this, training was huge for me. I pushed myself physically and mentally to prepare for this climb.

I took an old tire and drilled an eye hook through it to train with. I attached lashing straps and tied them to my backpack to learn how to pull weight. It turned out to be a good idea and an inexpensive way to prepare myself.

The Challenge Coin

As I ran one day as part of my training routine, I felt God was telling me to design a challenge coin. We often use these coins to foster a long-lasting bond between people. Everyone has a mountain to climb—a challenge in their life. Our challenge coins help guarantee that no one ever climbs alone.

I designed one for the Denali climb to hand out while training for the summit. God uses them to give me more opportunities to impact people on the trails and through interactions across the world. Often, I'd strike up a conversation with someone, get a good read on them, and challenge them to do X, Y, or Z. The challenge could be something critically important in their life, and really, it's between them and God if they complete it.

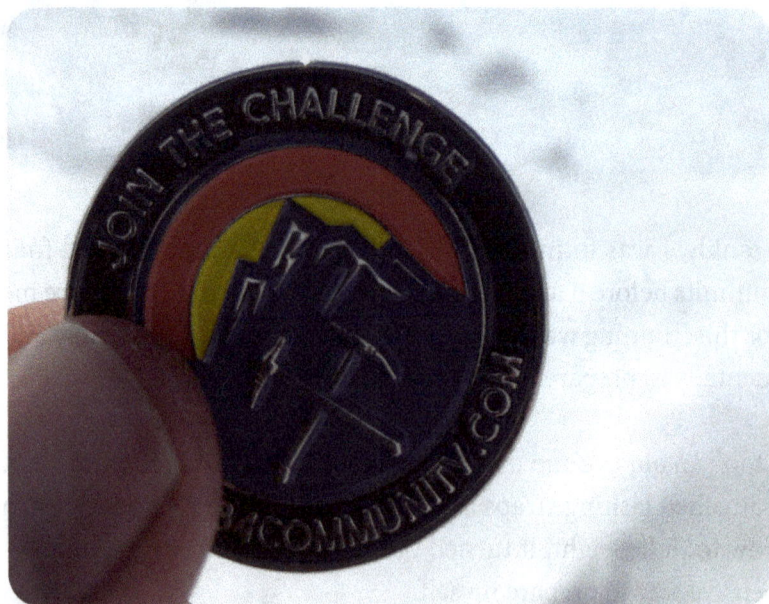

On the New Reach Foundation side, it marks Isaiah 41:1-3. That alone, led to starting many conversations with people while training for Denali. I may never know the impact these challenge coins have on everyone I give them to, but I feel God is doing something good through these small gifts. I believe having something with them as a tangible connection to a goal or challenge that they're striving for builds confidence. Climb for Community coins continue to be handed out across the world.

Get Ready

God was preparing me for this one. I made connections with the challenge coins while training, and then, about two weeks later, I went to a Christian worship day event. While I was basking in worship, He showed a very simple yet impactful visual.

While celebrating with my eyes closed, I simply saw an image of Jesus and I standing on the summit of North America together. I stood to his right, and He was holding my left hand. Our arms were outstretched upward in celebration.

I felt him saying, "Have fun with this one, Scott."

In the days leading up to this, I had been stretched, grown, and pushed, with uncertainty and desire swirling through me. It was a struggle to prepare for this trip, more so than the previous climbs.

During this time, Melanie and I felt we needed to prepare for what would be next. This message wasn't just for Denali but also for the next step in our lives. We both felt we were supposed to move. We needed a place that was more globally accessible. So, we listed our house for sale and started searching for a place within a reasonable distance from the airport.

I flew to Anchorage while Melanie dealt with the house. At the hotel, I met the team and felt connected to His plan immediately. There were crosses everywhere. He was letting me know everything was okay.

Then, I met with a slight moment of doubt when we entered a conference room at the hotel, with bins filled with candy bars. We "shopped" for our treats and food on the mountain from those bins. I'm thinking, "I don't eat this crap," but I shopped for next month's rations on the mountain and followed the path.

The equipment check came next, and that was different, too. I trusted the guide company, knowing they're top-notch. They didn't check the gear lightly, as many expedition companies do. They were serious about it, going over every piece and making sure it was what we needed and that it was functional.

Landing on a Glacier

The plane company owner flew us on an extraordinary flight with "extra" adventure. The twin otter with skis landed on the Kahiltna Glacier. Coming down between snowy peaks and landing on snow… was one of the most fun flights I've ever been on. We set up tents and ran some skills assessment drills right there on the glacier for the first day.

On day two, we got our sleds. I had close to 70 pounds in my backpack, plus another 30 to 40 pounds on my sled. We were roped together and had to stride together. In this environment, we had to be in rhythm as a team and really on our game so we didn't endanger one another.

Being roped together and working together to move up the mountain is parallel to managing a functioning team in business. How does the rope connect one person to the next? What does the rhythm look like? How are you in control of your own sled? How are you moving?

Beautiful and Deadly

We're wearing snowshoes on the approach for our first day on the move. We're on the ice, surrounded by an expansive mountain range. It's absolutely breathtaking but also deadly.

I'm in the middle of the rope team, and a good friend is behind me. My friend accidentally steps on the rope, pulling everyone back. The rope leader came down hard on us, and his temper immediately escalated. He's a tight leader, but he's got a good reason for being that way.

Moving a team together in unison is absolutely critical anywhere, but this is especially true in Denali. The crevasse danger is real. We cannot have equipment failures. Everyone must be on top of self-management, movement, and more. All these variables come into play for success or death in Denali.

Caching Your Gear

You have Camp One, Camp Two, and Camp Three to get through before you hit Base Camp at about 14,000 feet on the way to the summit. On Denali, we do what we call "caching gear."

We arrived at Camp One, and the next day, we took everything we needed to use up high on the mountain, halfway to Camp Two. We dug a big hole in the ice and put all our team gear in there. Everything we don't need until high in the mountain. We buried it and marked it.

Then, we moved back to Camp One. This accomplished two things. It helped us acclimate to the elevation and get used to the environment. It also lightened our load as we moved up the mountain.

Depending on the weather, you may typically rest for one or two days. After our break, we moved from Camp One to Camp Two and set up our tents. We completed what is called a "back carry" by going down to where we cached our gear, pulling it out of the hole we buried it in, and carrying it to Camp Two.

The next day, we moved our gear up between Camp Two and Camp Three. We had to repeat the process from Camp Three to Base Camp. At least, that was the plan.

The Wisdom of Leaders, The Arrogance of Teams

The carry forward, cache gear, and back carry process seemed like a lot of extra work. My buddy and I thought we could shave off a day on this back-and-forth packing routine and do it differently. Instead of caching our gear between Camp Three and Base Camp, we just carried it all the way to Base Camp. We're strong, the weather's great, no problem, we thought.

The team leaders (guides) didn't appreciate our ingenuity. The system exists for a reason–our safety. To make their point, they didn't give us the day of rest we'd hoped for by getting ahead of schedule. Instead, they used the extra day for more training and work. Lesson learned–don't change the system until you understand why the system exists.

An Unforgettable Summit

Base Camp is about 14,000 ft, and this was where we learned how the summit works. Right after Base Camp is the Headwall. This is the steepest part of Denali and the crux of the route. The last 800ft of the steep slope is made of ice with fixed ropes.

Going back to the challenge coins, I trained for this section on the Manitou Incline in Colorado. I was in my 8,000-meter boots, moving slowly like you would to replicate this Headwall. I ended up with quite a following there by handing out so many coins and building relationships with people during that training.

That training helped me feel super strong on the Headwall and gave me confidence. On my last headwall rotation, I climbed next to a father-daughter team who were also climbing the 7 Summits. They had just come off of climbing Everest. Watching that girl accept the Headwall challenge and how she learned the different climbing techniques was impressive. At one point, she said, "Wow, this is really hard," and that caught my attention, considering they had just come off of Everest.

After the Headwall is the 16 Ridge, where you cache your gear. We had to do that a few more times because of the weather, and we got stranded at Base Camp for five days. The weather rolled in fast. Some people made bad decisions at the top, and severe rescues were made for them. We were stuck, and we sawed the ice into blocks to build walls and shelter from the winds.

That Friday, we hunkered down in the tent, and I thought back to that image He gave me two weeks before the trip. Sunday is Father's Day, and I thought, how amazing would it be if we summit on Father's Day? Wow! That's what He really meant. The weather would lighten up, and I would summit with my Father. How cool was that?

It didn't happen. We couldn't move until one or two days after Father's Day. We moved in rope teams up the Headwall and onto 16 Ridge. Our three-person rope team was powerful and in sync with one another. That type of dependency on one another builds deep connections. One guy became my close buddy because of this trip, and the other was our lead assistant.

Be on Your Game

On 16 Ridge, it gets technical. You must pay attention and be on your game to navigate the environment. We had to do what's called running belays on the ice rock. You clip onto anchors and have to use good crampon techniques here, or you can pull your team off. Some areas are very dangerous, where famous stories of people dying took place.

The three of us loved it and had the time of our lives. In our excitement, we took all our team gear out of the cache and ran the ridgeline with the extra heavy packs, feeling like kids again. We got to the high camp a few hours earlier than the others.

Even though we carried everything, the three of us set up camp for everyone. I had a bit of a chip on my shoulder because we picked up the slack and didn't even get a "thank you."

After a day of rest, we headed toward the summit, first reaching an area called the Autobahn. It's a side hill where you clip yourself in and do a running belay. The path is only five or six inches wide. If you slip, it's a thousand-foot drop.

The name for this section was reportedly born out of tragedy. Years ago, three German climbers lost their lives because they weren't roped together correctly. Too many deadly falls have been reported on the Autobahn.

After we trekked through the Autobahn, we traversed a section called the Zebra Rocks. The name refers to the spectacular black and white rock faces that climbers zig-zag through. We were close to 19,000 ft, and the weather rolled in to steal our good mood after we moved through the Zebra Rocks.

Do We or Don't We?

We talked to people ahead of us on the radio, and they told us it was bad. We should turn around. My buddy was a little upset because he had missed this summit once before because of insufficient team dynamics. We had a group team discussion about whether to keep going or turn back around.

It was a tough choice. We could keep going forward and know we won't have another shot at it if we don't make it. Or, we could go back down and wait out the weather to make another attempt to summit. I stayed quiet because of my past experiences while my buddy explained his frustration.

Ultimately, we turned around, and I got sick when we returned to camp—really sick. People said it was just altitude sickness, and I denied it, already falling back on the tricks of the trade I learned on the Aconcagua climb.

After much discussion, my tentmate and I planned on leaving the next day for another attempt. I was getting sicker by the minute. I had concerns about high-altitude pulmonary edema. I was spitting up blood and not feeling right; however, I still had the strength and determination to continue. I knew my limits and felt confident I could push through, keeping a close eye on how I was feeling.

We'll Try Again

After we let the weather ease, we ended up with two rope teams. Our team led the way.

When you climb, you have to be careful not to be a risk to everyone else by compromising the team dynamics. My own personal assessment was that I was good to go. I felt in tune with the climb.

I wasn't slowing anybody down and did not feel like I would be a risk.

I always try to put other people first, so, in confidence, I told my buddy to watch me. As a lifeline, I wanted him to keep an eye on me as an outside observer.

At the Autobahn, we got behind some really slow people, which can make or break a day because they are inexperienced. They did not know what they were doing and made mistakes. We stopped moving, and the cold settled in, which made my situation worse.

While traversing the Zebra Rocks, I had a moment of fear. I looked back at the rock face behind me and thought I could have high-altitude cerebral edema at that point. I've had brain swell before, so I was familiar with how it felt.

Again, I was still moving fine. I wasn't slowing anything down. I was 99% aware and behaving okay. Even my outside observer said I wasn't stumbling and looked perfectly fine. So, we kept moving.

Finally, we reached a long park section called the Football Field. I felt awful. I prayed and sought His help, talking to Jesus and praying to get through this.

Not long after, we reached a hill called Pig Hill right before the summit ridge. Someone was sick and held everyone up during this part of the climb. We couldn't move for around 45 minutes, and we became frustrated. Upon reflection, I believe that may have been part of His plan so I could collect myself and push forward through my sickness.

I made it up Pig Hill, absolutely miserable, and I felt 100% worse pushing up the summit ridge. I can't remember much about the summit experience. I was just too sick. We took the summit photo, people high-fived our achievement, and there was a medallion on the summit. I remember little more than that. Denali's summit is 6,194 meters/20,320 feet. However, the difference in barometric pressure due to latitude affects the summit, which "feels" closer to 6,900 meters/22,000 feet.

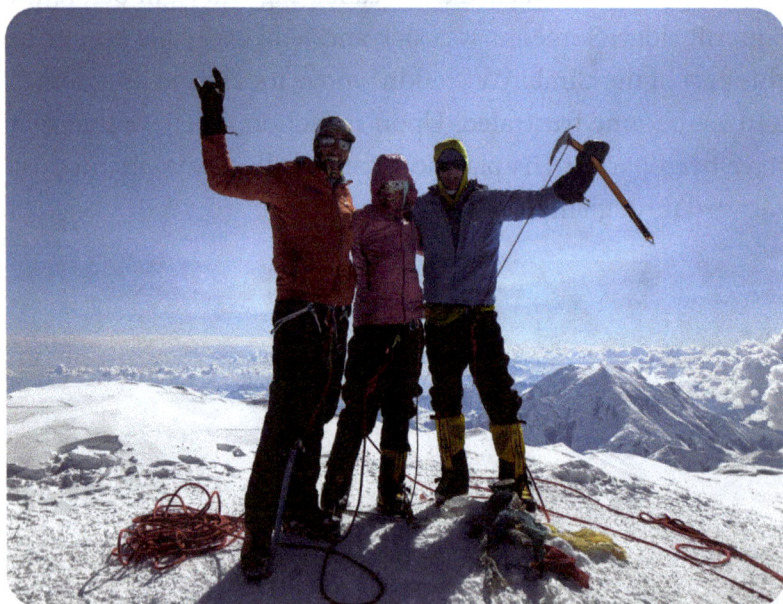

The Death March

Coming down was worse—much worse. I was a total wreck. I was moving fine, and everything was going well, but I didn't feel okay. Everyone said I looked well and very strong all this time.

How many times does this happen in life? You can feel horrible, physically or mentally, yet no one around you can tell that you're going through some trauma on the inside. How often do we miss seeing the suffering of others because we don't look deep enough?

On the way down, I completely surrendered at one spot. It was a fall-to-my-knees moment of pure surrender. "I can't do this without you, Jesus. I can't do this on my own. I need you."

We got back down to High Camp, and I was done. My team gave me ramen noodles, and it was the best meal I have ever had in my life. At this point, people were still saying I had AMS and that I would get better the lower we went. I didn't think so. By the time we arrived back in Base Camp, I was worse. I lay in a tent, feeling miserable and much, much worse. In the end, I had pneumonia. I summited through pneumonia.

We hung out at camp for a little while, and then I walked the Death March all the way to the plane. It's a long and dangerous climb down, and you keep going throughout the night. It was a miserable time for me.

So, What Does This Mean?

It goes back to that image two weeks before I left on the trip. I'm standing on the summit with Jesus. I thought it meant He was telling me to have fun. Do you remember the raised arms and Him holding my hand? Well, He was not telling me to have fun.

There was absolutely no way I could make it on my strength alone. It was that relationship with Him that carried me through. I looked and moved fine to others on this dangerous climb, but I only got through it by fully surrendering to Him.

It took me going through this struggle and not getting through it without Him to see the truth of this image. There's no way I could do this on my own strength. The stamp of *relationship* was marked on this climb during my moment of complete surrender.

The Relationship is the Key

We build bridges to create relationships. The bridge helps us connect with our team and the people within our range of influence. It starts with authenticity.

People are smart. They know when they are being manipulated. Today's leaders can be misaligned with the right way to lead. Leadership is a role of continued growth, continual learning, and understanding. We create a real impact when we recognize our capacity to be a good leader and strive toward that.

Now, we have this framework of these four other pillars where it all happens, much like my relationship with Christ. We start believing and taking these steps when we're in that relationship. We do crazy things like leave our jobs and climb the 7 Summits.

Everything comes down to one word—*relationship*. We have the first four lessons and *relationship* is where we get to share that with other people. Relationships build communities and respect. It will happen in the workplace, in marriage, parenting, mentoring, friendships, everything.

Lack of relationship weakens communities, culture, and our legacy. We cannot go further on our journey and discover what "more" is available for us without relationship. **Relationship is the key to achieving the "more"—it's a requirement.**

You're building a bridge to greater things—more possibilities—when you create relationships with others through intentional conversations and your beliefs. The relationship will add clarity to your conversations and impact the results.

Listen, trust, be open. Be in the relationship and respond to what you're asked to do.

CHAPTER 6

Mt. Vinson - Choose Joy

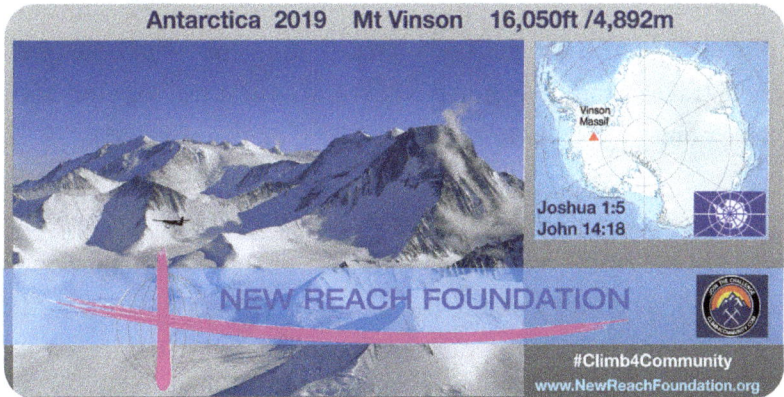

Antarctica 2019   Mt Vinson   16,050ft /4,892m

Joshua 1:5
John 14:18

NEW REACH FOUNDATION

#Climb4Community
www.NewReachFoundation.org

"No man shall be able to stand before you all the days of your life. Just as I was with Moses, so I will be with you. I will not leave you or forsake you."
Joshua 1:5

Joy doesn't happen to you—it is not happiness. It is a state of being joyful in whatever role you find yourself in each day. You make a conscious choice to live within these lessons and share that gift with others.

Mt. Vinson is the highest mountain in Antarctica, with a summit of 4,892 meters/16,050 feet. It's one of the most remote locations in the world. Vinson is extremely challenging to get to and is only open for climbing five weeks of the year. It is a cold, untouched territory—and breathtakingly beautiful.

The Trip to the Bottom of the Earth

My years of traveling so much for work before my 7 Summits journey became a blessing. I racked up a lot of points from those travels, and I feel honored to be able to travel for God with these points.

They gave me a little financial push, but this 7 Summits journey was still costly. Mt. Vinson was one of the biggest monetary challenges. This climb was the most expensive thus far before Mt. Everest, and the $7,000 down payment nearly wiped me out. Luckily, an unexpected check arrived just in time to pay for the rest of this trip.

Mt. Vinson is deceiving because the stats make it look achievable compared to other climbs around the world. After all I learned on Denali, it didn't appear to be as difficult. I felt confident with my experience and ability to climb this mountain. I trained, but I was honestly less polished in my efforts than before.

To get there, you have to travel to Punta Arenas in the southern part of Chile. I went by way of Buenos Aires to stay with one of my tentmates from Aconcagua, building on that relationship. I knew it would risk using extra time, but it brought more opportunity for community and impact. As it happened, there were riots in Santiago, Chile, and I was stranded for a bit. That delayed me getting to Punta Arenas, and I barely made it within the ideal weather window for this trip.

An Exclusive and Unique Flight

We flew to the Union Glacier in Antarctica by way of a Russian cargo plane, the Ilyushin Il-76, which was an awesome experience. Only certain pilots are trained to go there and the Russian cargo plane is being replaced by Icelandair Trip 7.

The expeditions are limited to five weeks a year because Mt Vinson is still extremely remote, and very few people can go to climb there. There is only one group each week, and everyone that climbs that week flies there together. They scatter the climbing teams so they don't all go up at the same time, but everyone flies to Union Glacier together.

The Blue Ice Runway

We took the cold 5 ½ hour flight to Union Glacier on the huge, Ilyushin Il-76–a noisy military cargo plane. The unique landing on the blue ice runway added to the excitement of visiting such a unique place. Instead of using brakes to slow down, the aircraft used reverse thrusters to slide to a stop. The cargo plane had no windows, further throwing our senses off and creating a surreal landing experience. To land on this runway, pilots must be specially certified. It's not your average airport.

The blue ice runway at Union Glacier remains nearly snow-free. Air bubbles get forced out in this environment, and the ice density increases. The surface strengthens enough to allow aircraft to land with wheels instead of skis.

We landed at 2:00 AM under a startlingly bright sky. Our jaws dropped at the magnificent view as we descended the ladder onto the blue ice runway. The spectacular mountain range surrounding us just took our breath away. The entire panoramic view was completely white—it felt like we went to a white Mars on Earth. It's beautiful. It's untouched. It's magnificent.

Mt. Vinson's Unique Approach

Our transportation from the runway to the Union Glacier Base Camp were these Tucker Sno-Cats and 6-wheel drive vehicles modified for polar operations. Riding in these vehicles is a very unique, exhilarating experience, especially the Tucker Sno-Cats.

Their articulating 4-track system allows them to handle the unique geography of the area. Before each season, they go out and map out the routes with GPS for the five-week climbing season, so when you travel, you follow those points very closely.

The base camp is a unique full-service village of clamshell tents where every little need has been thought through. They even fly out these huge restroom units just for the season. The heart of the camp is the dining tent, where chefs serve a wide range of foods.

Always Ready To Go

When it comes to climbing mountains, climbers always have to be in a "ready...go!" mindset. That's how it was for us after landing on the blue ice. No one told us who our guides were or when we would leave. We hung out in the dining tent for a brief snack, and then suddenly, we were told we were leaving. No time to prepare or gather details...we just grabbed our gear and went.

A twin otter flew us 95 miles to the Vinson Base Camp, and the view from the plane was overwhelming. The majestic, snow-covered peaks of the Sentinel Range rose up over vast glaciers below us as we flew through untouched territory, places where people don't go... Where we shouldn't be going. It was such a privilege.

The Vinson Base Camp is only accessible by the ski planes like the one that took us. It's a more basic version of Union Glacier Camp, and we were to meet in the mess tent after settling into our tents. For the first time in my life, I was late. I hadn't slept for days and was so exhausted from my trip that I closed my eyes after unpacking.

I arrived late for the briefing. If you know me, you know me as Mr. Punctual. I believe if you're not 10 minutes early, you're late. Everyone was so pissed at me, and it was the last time I made that mistake.

Base Camp to Camp One

We put on harnesses for the hike to Camp One and roped off into three-person teams. There are a lot of crevasses, and we need to work together to ensure no one falls into them. My rope partners were an elite-level athlete from Africa and a guide.

The sun never goes down there, so we left at a very specific time. A rock face helps block out the sun for part of the climb. Even though we timed it for safety and it was super cold (-40 degrees), I still gave myself a heat stroke.

The sun radiated off the ice and blasted heat into us. I fought through the headaches and nausea during this section. To make matters more miserable, my African partner kept stopping, unable to keep the rhythm. It was a relief to make Camp Two and get beyond that frustration.

Camp One to Camp Two

Going to Camp Two is much like the Denali Headwall but more challenging. We rope climbed across a steep section with a lot of external factors to deal with. One minute, the sun reflected heat off the snow; the next, we're freezing in the -40-degree air. Blue ice is everywhere—harder than cement, and kicking crampons into it is challenging.

When we reached Camp Two, we were rewarded with some magnificent views. The frozen, beautiful landscape of the towering snow-capped peaks really made it feel as if we were on the edge of the world. When we left Camp Two, I felt honored to be there as we traversed a giant field on our way to Summit Ridge.

Pushing to the Summit

Summit Ridge is a beautiful ridgeline, and when we got there, I thought, "I wish this was longer." I was in a state of peace, thinking, "I want to enjoy this. I am having fun."

I don't think I've ever felt joyful. I am more of a serious guy. I struggle with people who are always smiling and laughing. Yet, at the summit, He stamped the word *joy* onto my journey.

The weather was great. I was just basking in the joy of the summit, which is so contrary to my nature. I'm usually the run fast, run hard, Type A guy, and this climb allowed me to see how choosing joy in my life will help me build better relationships and do greater things for those around me.

On Mt. Vinson, He showed me the power of making a choice through that joy. I could choose to wallow in the negativity of the world, or I could use the power of *joy* to engage the lessons I've learned so far on this journey. Not happiness. Joy is something much more profound. Joy is a way of life. We can choose to strive for joy every single day.

I had to travel to a remote place like Antarctica to understand, experience, and feel joy. To see what it means. Joy is a game changer, and I experienced it on the ridgeline. It was a great summit day with beautiful weather and an amazing top-of-the-world view to take in.

Stranded at Base Camp

Descending Mount Vinson was uneventful for us, not that I didn't try to make it more exciting. I wanted to do this other climb that people don't usually get to do. Unfortunately, the guide wasn't available.

Two significant factors played a role in why this climb's ending didn't go as planned.

At the same time we're taking this trip, a Chilean Air Force military transport plane en route to Antarctica crashed, killing everyone aboard. People at home thought we may have been on that plane and didn't know if we made it. So, we had to deal with that on our return to Base Camp.

We were more impacted by how that plane crash led to the Ilyushin Il-76 being grounded in Chile for critical inspection. They would only allow it to fly and return for us once that inspection was carried out. So, we returned to Union Glacier and became stranded for five days. There's no way out, and nothing's coming in. The reactions of the climbers were not what I expected.

As you know, Mount Vinson is an extremely expensive climb. Three types of climbers go to Mt Vinson. Some save their entire life for the trip, while others take it on as part of the 7 Summits and find a way. Then, there are those who can simply write a check without a moment's hesitation.

We were well taken care of at the Union Glacier Camp. The food was great, and we were in the middle of this big, beautiful white playground. The 7 Summit climbers and those who used their life savings to get there were basking in the adventure.

Some people were in an uproar. Their chests were puffed up with pride and indignation at being told they couldn't leave. They were rude to our attentive guides, yelling and screaming. "We're going to get our private planes to come in here!" Of course, that's not allowed, which only made them throw bigger tantrums.

I had signed up with Antarctic Logistics Expeditions (ALE), the main company running everything. While a few of the more affluent tried to gain control, ALE took us out in specialized ice vehicles. We explored, climbed other mountains, ice climbed, and rode mountain bikes. We got to do all this fun stuff. We had a blast.

I also spent a lot of time in the library in quiet prayer. God kept placing new steps for the New Reach Foundation on my heart, and I took notes on more ways we could positively impact the world.

I also started to see the role the 7 Summits played on my journey—why He sent me to climb mountains. What better way to fulfill my purpose of helping others through the foundation than taking it across the world? God chose seven mountains on seven continents because God's people are on every continent.

He blessed me by allowing me to make it back on December 24th, just in time for my son's birthday on the 25th.

Joy is a Choice

Joy is a choice. Every day, we face the ability to say yes or no to joy.

As managers and executives, we make about 3 billion decisions each year.[2] Cornell University estimated that we make 226.7 decisions each day on food alone.[3] As your level of responsibility increases, so does the number of choices you make. You may make 35,000 choices a day![4]

Joy doesn't just happen. You choose to have joy in your life. You choose whether to experience joy every single day.

[2] The University of North Carolina at Chapel Hill . (2023, June 26). *Decision-making strategies for business success.* UNC. https://onlinemba.unc.edu/news/decision-making-strategies-for-business-success/

[3] Hoomans, Dr. J. (2015, March 20). *35,000 decisions: The great choices of strategic leaders.* Roberts Wesleyan College. https://go.roberts.edu/leadingedge/the-great-choices-of-strategic-leaders

[4] Krockow, E. (2018, September 27). *How many decisions do we make each day?.* Psychology Today. https://www.psychologytoday.com/us/blog/stretching-theory/201809/how-many-decisions-do-we-make-each-day

Where do we find our joy? How do we get it? Do we even know what it means? These are the questions you'll answer on your journey.

I discovered penetrating joy when in this place that was untouched, pure, white—a place that seemed as if no human should ever invade. Amidst this almost nothingness, I understood what joy meant to me.

Joy is a thing...it's not happiness. It's deep within us, and we all show it differently. Some people just exude joy as they walk down the street. You can see it and feel it radiating off of them without them saying a word. Others, like me, carry joy way down deep inside of ourselves. You don't see it on the outside, but it comes out through our passion.

Just as having joy is a choice, how you experience your joy is a very personal thing. How you discover your joy and what it means to you is uniquely yours. Everyone has the capacity to experience joy in their life. You only have to choose to open your heart and mind to it.

To find joy, you must let go of self-defeating thoughts. "I'm not happy. I'm not joyful because…" You can't control the circumstances 100% of the time. Joy exists outside of your current circumstances. It is the result of you making a decision. You get to consciously choose joy.

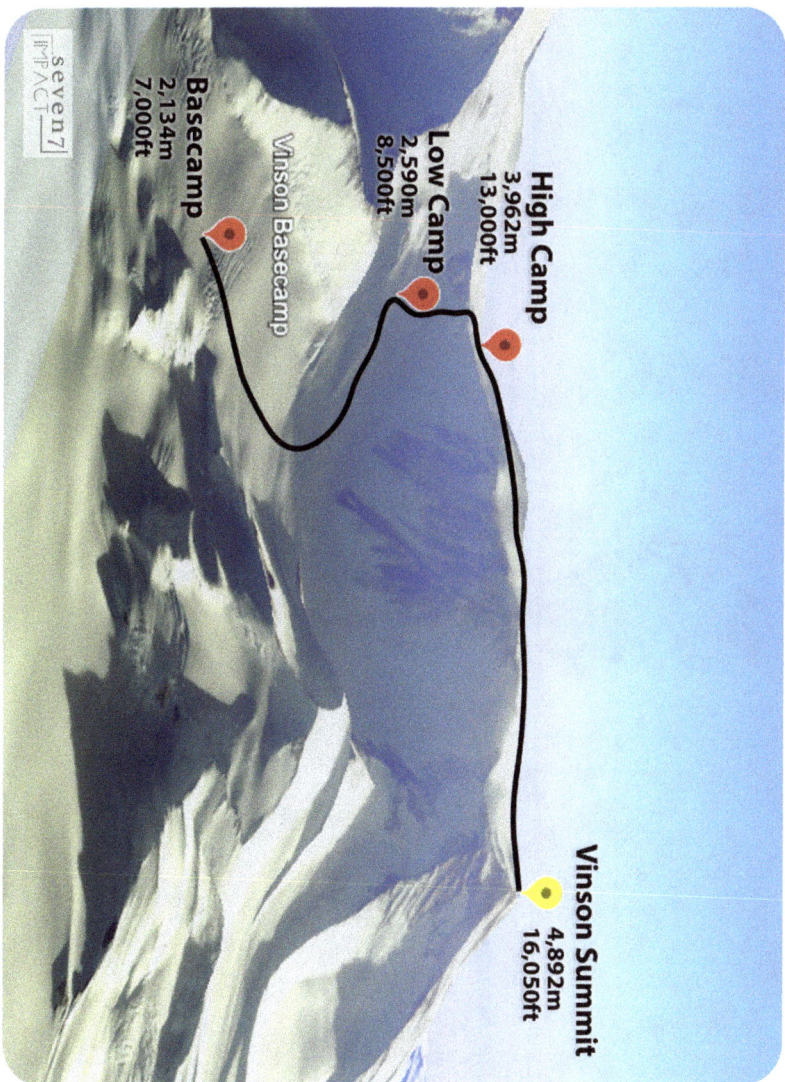

High Camp
3,962m
13,000ft

Low Camp
2,590m
8,500ft

Vinson Basecamp

Basecamp
2,134m
7,000ft

Vinson Summit
4,892m
16,050ft

seven7
IMPACT

CHAPTER 7

Everest - You Will Have Manna

*"For behold, he who forms the mountains and creates
the wind, and declares to man what is his thought, who
makes the morning darkness, and treads on the heights
of the earth-- the LORD, the God of hosts, is his name!"*
Amos 4:13

**Manna represents being supplied with what you need to meet
the challenge you're called to face today. Then trusting that you
will be resupplied tomorrow and the next day.**

Mount Everest is the climb that everyone's heard about. It's the Earth's highest mountain, with a summit of 8,848 meters/29,031 feet. This final summit in my 7 Summits challenge proved to be a monumental task—physically, financially, mentally, and in travel.

Disruptions at the Start

Mount Everest was on our list for 2020, and we heard about the outbreak of COVID-19 in China in December 2019. We planned around it by building our team and communicating to control the situation.

Then, six days before I was to leave for Everest in March 2020, the world shut down. After working so long to prepare mentally and physically, I had to stop everything. Right from the beginning, Everest was a different kind of challenge.

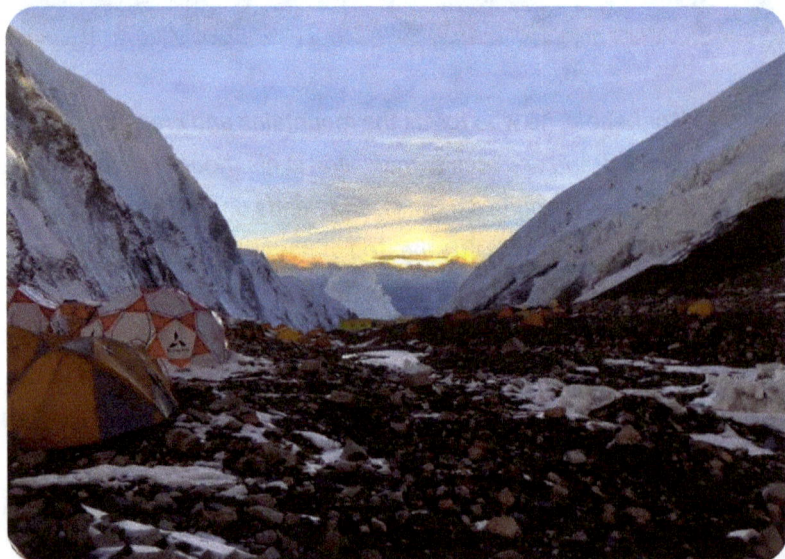

The Enemy at Work

The 7 Summit journey showed me how to overcome the challenges in front of me through God's strength. The closer I got to putting this whole journey together, the more disruptions the enemy put in my path. The more obstacles that built up to stop me from completing my mission, the more I worked to release control and face those challenges head-on.

The sickness taking over the world felt like a spiritual attack, and that told me something big was happening. When I couldn't go to Nepal, I knew this journey was bigger than I thought. I was ready to get there at any cost, but my options were limited. Climbing Everest would have to wait.

I had to wait for another year to get to Everest and maintain my conditioning. For the whole of 2020, I trained, prepared, and conditioned for the climb. Mentally and spiritually, it was one of my most challenging times. I felt my whole life was put on hold until this was completed.

Changing the Plan of Attack

The two most commonly used routes to summit Mount Everest are via Nepal or Tibetan China. We planned to climb Everest from the Tibetan side in China, but in 2021, China still wasn't open. We adjusted everything to climb from the Nepalese side instead.

Climbing Everest during COVID-19 added chaos to the challenges already associated with climbing this mountain. Wearing masks was mandatory, and we needed a negative COVID test to enter the Khumbu region. There was sickness everywhere, and differing opinions on how to deal with the illness affected everything. People across Nepal were making poor decisions, people were stressed, and people were dying from COVID throughout the region.

We made sure the pandemic did not stop us from visiting remote villages in search of New Reach Foundation projects. On every trip, we meet the local people, share love in various ways, and understand the culture to discover new ways we can help.

The dust and pollution impacted my throat and asthmatic lungs significantly and put me at risk starting this climb, leaving me with a bad cough.

The pandemic influenced people and businesses throughout the area, causing us to make last-minute judgment calls about our travel. We decided to fly from Kathmandu to a small town called Namche Bazaar to get ahead and distance ourselves. Trouble is, that flight was nearly a 7,000 foot elevation change, which means we lost the benefit of acclimation that would have come from hiking in. The higher altitude hit me hard, thanks to the throat issues I already had from the visits to the villages.

Too Many Unknowns and Uncertainty

When traveling to these places, staying in tea houses full of people is customary. Not this time. All the tea houses were eerily deserted. Usually, these areas are so alive and vibrant. Instead, we encountered bad vibes everywhere and sad faces of devastated people whose misery we were invading.

It definitely took me out of my comfort zone. I just did my best to let go, trust God, and move forward on this journey, looking for any small opportunity to make a difference. It was rough and a bit overwhelming to witness such despair.

Our team leaders were juggling a lot of new decisions as a result of the pandemic restrictions on the mountain. We had two top-notch guides who were among the best, and even they couldn't agree on how to deal with certain situations we encountered on this climb. As someone who experiences the culture and people on these trips, seeing people during a uniquely rough time in their lives was difficult.

Opportunists and Corruption

You hear all the time that people pay their way up Everest. It's easy for the wealthy to get to climb this mountain, even if they have no business being there. Everest has so many unqualified climbers, and that risks lives. They cause the most dangerous bottlenecks and stoppages at the high points.

Typically, these unqualified climbers get sick, and some die. Some summit only because the Sherpas are such amazing people, but they can only do so much. During our trip, too many people on the climb were making poor decisions.

Witnessing how people traded the quality of the climb and people's lives for money saddened me. People climbed even though they had COVID-19. Many were encouraged to hide their symptoms, and there were rumors of people paying for fake negative COVID-19 tests.

Bad decisions cost the Sherpas dearly. It was the first time that Sherpas dropped dead at high altitude. Sherpas fell into crevasses in known territories due to the overload of stress, causing them not to be as aware and agile and perhaps from feeling the effects of COVID-19 themselves.

Heading to Base Camp

We went from tea house to tea house and village to village to acclimate and make our way to Base Camp. It was a long ten or twelve-day trip. We experienced several Puja ceremonies at some of the special temples along the route to be blessed by the Buddhists.

The altitude gain on this trek is 2,504 meters/8,215 feet, beginning in an alpine forest and ending in the camp's frozen world. We climbed over a moraine from the famous Everest Base Camp

Rock and down some ice to get into Base Camp. Our sherpa teams arrived before us and had everything set up in this beautiful area. I could look up at the Khumbu Icefall from outside my tent.

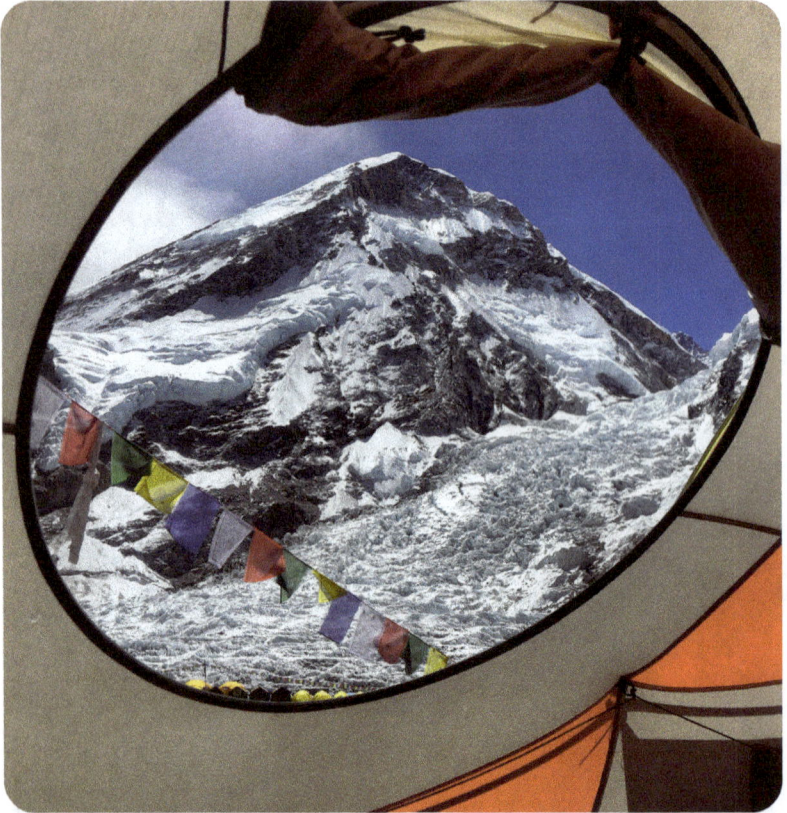

My tent sat on the uneven glacier, where the ice was slowly melting around us. The ground beneath us would crack, and the constant sound of avalanches echoed around us. Vast sections of ice and snow would break away as the terrain shifted, and I couldn't shake the feeling that I was stepping right into the heart of this powerful place.

The Icefall Doctors is a group of some of the bravest sherpas who risk their lives so we can climb Mount Everest. These doctors construct and maintain a safe passage through the icefall for the climbers every year. Armed with ropes and ladders, they bridge deep crevasses to secure the route and then stay to maintain them throughout the climbing season. The icefall constantly shifts, and at any point, one of the ice towers can collapse, along with avalanche risks any time.

We were isolated. Climbing authorities restricted us and told us we couldn't do anything with the other climbers. People went up and down in rotations to acclimate, and that's when people started getting sick. The Nepalese government will probably never admit there was COVID-19 in the camp to this day, but there certainly was rampant sickness like no other year.

It was impossible to control everything, but we tried. We went out on acclimating hikes. Our team spread out on the Khumbu to run assessment drills and brush up on our climbing and ice skills. Whatever we could do to keep our team ready for the summit.

Being Thankful

A high priest came in for a Puja ceremony. He performed the scrolling prayers, blessed the equipment we brought to them, and asked for positive things from Buddha for us in this beautiful ceremony. It was a beautiful ceremony to witness. I could feel the powerful influence of their beliefs and the love of their people.

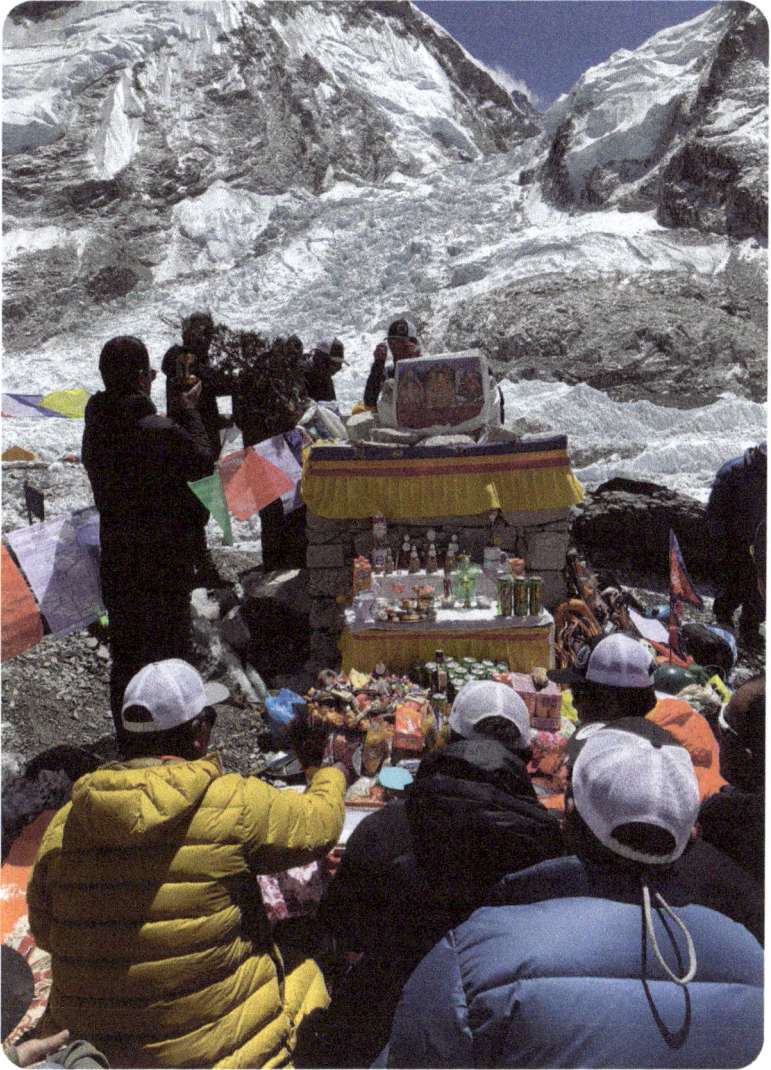

While the ceremony happened, I prayed to Jesus. I thanked Him for these people, for everything. Very few get to feel the wonder of being with these people, celebrating part of their lives and who they are. It's a gift I'm thankful for.

We Head Into the Khumbu

As we headed into the icefall at 2:00 am, moonbeams radiated off the ice, and I forgot about the dangers amidst its beauty. And that's where our team dynamic fell completely apart. We started with seven climbers, a lead guide, an assistant guide, and two Sherpas going with us as we elevated.

A climber from Canada became ill. A Westerner and a Sherpa left with a radio to take her down. This left us with one Sherpa, a guide, and one radio. We moved forward without a radio at the back. Our team spread out, and we lost communication with one another. A good friend of mine fell back, and we lost him. Soon, we were down to five climbers and a guide and spreading out more. Eventually, the lead guide stayed back with two climbers and the sherpa was with a slower climber. Three of six (two at the front and one at the back) remaining climbers were left climbing in the most volatile environment on our own, unaccompanied by experienced guides.

Our lead guide fell back with someone else, and then I led the two of us who remained up the Khumbu. Somehow, we got to Camp One through a place we had never been before through an unpredictable environment.

Now what? We did not know where to go and had no means of communication. My buddy fell sick, and I felt the sickest I had ever felt. I had symptoms of AMS, severe headaches, and major GI issues. We finished the rotation, went down, did the second rotation, and then made it to Camp Two.

At Camp Two, two Sherpas tested positive on the second rotation. We opted to do the right thing and follow protocol. We returned to Base Camp and quarantined.

Lessons Learned From Poor Leadership

We got out of quarantine before the last summit rotation. We went down to 14,000 ft to let our bodies recover before the big summit push. On the way, I got angry. The leaders were on edge and not being leaders in any fashion. I thought about the mistakes made and the lessons we can learn from them.

Lesson 1:

I was on a Western team, and the mistakes in leadership on this climb really became evident when we did our first rotation in the Khumbu Icefall. Some critical decisions were made that could have led to fatalities. Three of us climbers went through the icefall unguided and unsupported, and that should have never happened.

This was very dangerous and unhealthy. It affects our health by spiking cortisol and other things, creating a high-stress level. You don't feel the stress, and that in itself becomes unsafe. Poor leadership just puts people in stages of stress that hinder their health and performance as a team.

Lesson 2:

Another leadership mistake happened on the second rotation in the Khumbu Icefall while we were moving up the mountain. In this case, I was behind the leader, and he was a poor communicator. I had to switch gears and rely on myself, not on him to guide me. A good leader enables, empowers, and gives control over to the people they lead.

Lesson 3:

We had just finished our second rotation and were leaving Everest Base Camp to come down lower to recover before our summit attempt. This is just below 18,000 feet. Some people go all the way to Kathmandu, but we didn't. Instead, we descended to a town called Dingboche (approx 14,000 feet).

The way down was a long trek, and part of our team became separated. The leadership was deplorable and non-existent. One guide raced off, and the other guide complained about stepping back to be with two slower folks. Neither guide had a pulse on team members or tracking correct trails to our tea house. I stepped up to manage the team as required to ensure safety and maintain others' location and pace. A servant leader steps up when it's required.

Lesson 4:

We had two world-class climbers who were supposed to be our leaders, but they were too busy fighting each other to be effective leaders. This greatly affected team morale in an already stressful environment and was very uncomfortable. World-class leaders fight battles alongside each other, not against one another.

It was a mess, and we stayed at 14,000 ft for a few days. I have a mission mentally - I can do anything for a month, anything for a week, anything for a day... However, this trip was different. I started the trip into Sagarmatha National Park with a severe cough from being out in villages before climbing, experienced AMS, had frantic long nights not being able to breathe, and experienced overall team frustrations. I kept focusing on getting through each day, and one thought kept coming back to me: I would be supplied with what I needed on a daily basis to get through each day.

Aiming for the Summit

Despite all of the above lessons, I trusted our leaders with our summit strategy. I had never seen so much helicopter activity for transporting climbers before. People would get sick, make poor decisions, and risk the lives of others for a shot at the summit. Some of my friends included. A couple were medevaced out before making it to the summit. This was a season of unusually high helicopter usage to get sick people out quickly. Helicopters were even used to advance certain climbers to avoid the risks of climbing up through an icefall or back down the icefall. This is simply another example of this misuse of medical resources for rescue aid. In fact, most people will disqualify a "summit" if the climber does not fully ascend and descend the complete mountain on their own merits.

There are typically two summit windows for the South Side of Everest. Oftentimes, the less experienced and less trained typically go in that early window. Early season risks are colder temperatures, less consistent days for the weather to hold, and bottlenecks typically caused by summit fever and low-budget teams chasing the opportunity. My team strategically planned to go up during the second window. As part of our risk management strategy, we let the reckless climbers go up and come off the mountain. This can add additional components of danger to the route.

Our summit attempt was going to be on May 21st. We worked with information from our weather reports and kept our strategy within risk management parameters. We never compromised safety protocols.

Others, like a couple of my friends, gave in to summit fever. They went up with sickness when they shouldn't have. They were going to do it no matter what it took, even if it cost them their life or endangered the lives of others. We had the tightest team on the climb at that time, even though the situation often stole our leaders away. We stayed within the tolerances, and the weather kept pushing out our summit window.

The 21st moved to the 22nd, then to the 23rd, then the 24th, and finally to the 25th. On the 25th, the game's over. It would be too dangerous because the icefall is like a cup of ice melting, constantly shifting everything. The mountain becomes more volatile, and the route changes, and this year, it was a much longer route than usual, with more risk of collapses and avalanches in the Khumbu.

It's Not Just Our Lives

The Nepalese government kept pushing the summit window open beyond the safe times and into the times it would be the most dangerous. The Icefall Doctors were forced to risk their lives every day to maintain and change the route. People did summits on the last day of May and maybe the first day of June, but we didn't.

Put yourself in our shoes. You're sitting in a tent at Base Camp. Think of everything you've worked for, spent time on, and trained so hard to accomplish. Every day, the weather is getting worse. Thoughts of the summit have built up through the anxiety among the members, the chaos, and the unknowns, and now, there may be an opportunity.

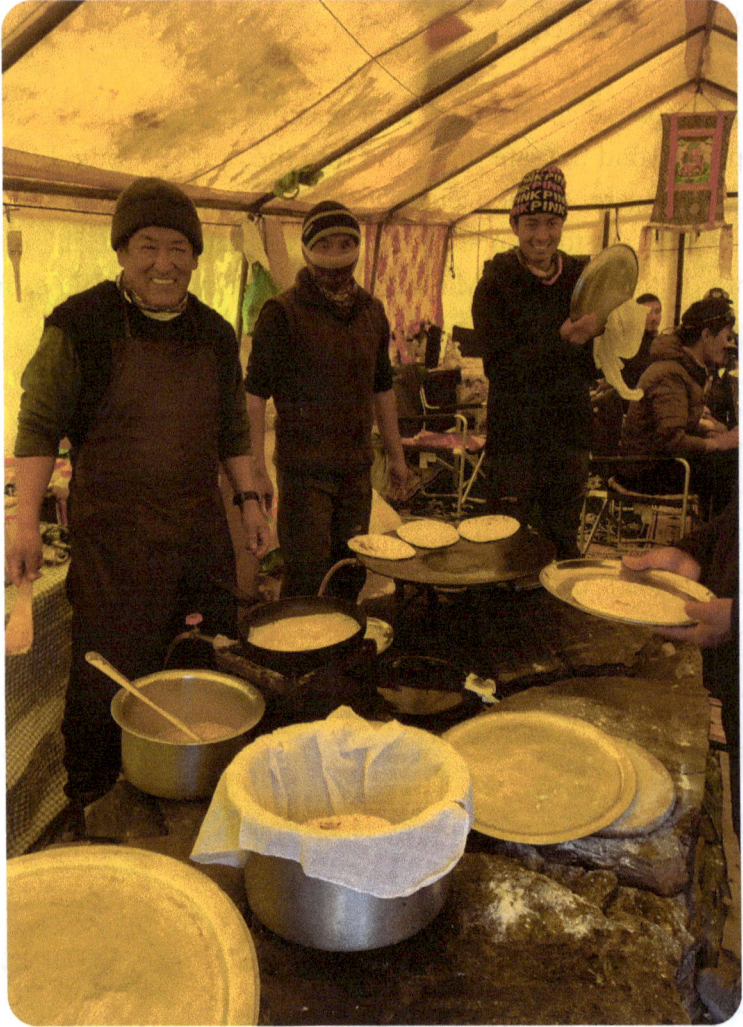

We had a decision to make as a team, and our decision was based on factors that many others didn't think about. We have gear at Camp Two, stuff at Camp Three, and more at Camp One. The day we summit, Sherpas must go up and down several times over days to bring all that gear down.

We do not do all that work. We only have the 40-pound packs on our backs. As time passed, conditions worsened, and we asked ourselves one question. Will we look our Sherpas in the eyes and ask them to sacrifice their lives to continue getting our gear for our summit?

We've already asked them to do that by waiting a few days. Now, the risk is hundreds of times greater. As a team, we chose not to ask this of our Sherpas.

"This is my commandment. That you love one another as I have loved you. Greater love has no one than this. That someone lay down his life for his friends."
John 15:12-15

Even though we weren't going to summit, I wholeheartedly felt I completed the ask He presented to me. I climbed the mountain, and I put others before me. There were a number of lives I helped save without getting one thank you, and that is okay. A good servant leader who puts others first every day will create the most positive impact. How powerful would that be if everyone did that every day?

The summit photo of Everest became the best photo because we're standing there with the Sherpas. Everyone is smiling and alive. We achieved something great that day because we didn't put their lives at risk.

The Stamp of Manna

The word *Manna* was marked on this mountain during a time over a month into our trip. There were seven distinct days when I didn't sleep well in a tent, which I still hate. I could not breathe. It was extremely claustrophobic, and I was scared.

I was trying to get through the night, fighting to be filled with whatever I needed to get through it. I kept hearing, "I'll give you what you need every day." And God provided. For example, in this case, one of the lead guides helped me get the Nepalese Flonase equivalent from supplies transported by helicopter to me…at Camp 2, nearly 22,000 ft. That is amazing.

Throughout this trip, everything kept adding up and stressing me out more each day. I believed I could do anything for a day, knowing He'd give me what I needed to get through it. During the worst moments, I believed I could do anything for just ten minutes. He would supply what I needed to get through. *Manna* was with me through all the chaos of this trip.

With that self-talk of how I can get through anything for a day, I made it, but this trip will stay with me for a long time. In fact, it haunted me for at least a year afterward. It was the disruptions in leadership and the people making poor decisions. It was my friends putting other people at risk. It was experiencing the local corruption and covering up, for what, money and acknowledgment. How often do we do the same?

Back to Kathmandu

Hiking back down was not as culturally enjoyable as it should have been. We frog-hopped our way down in a helicopter—tea houses were closed, everything was closed. The communities were still isolated and dealing with all the people dying from the sickness and in fear of more.

The world sickness was in full swing, and Kathmandu was closed. No one was coming in or getting out. Finally, the United States brought in a charter plane, and we could get back home. This US "charter plane" had only a few Americans on it, which came at a very high cash price. Lo and behold, this flight was full of Nepalese heading to our layover connection in Qatar. Need I say more.

So, What's the Point?

God is going to give you what you need every day. That is *Manna*. Everest taught me the critical importance of good leadership. Good leadership comes from making your decisions from the perspective of loving your neighbor.

Live within His words in John 15 and use those to guide you to continually grow and improve your leadership skills. Leadership skills that focus on the people your actions affect instead of just on the profit. When you operate under the guiding words God placed on the 7 Summits journey, you positively impact your life and those around you.

CHAPTER 8

Return to Everest - Living in the Pillars

"5-8 Those who think they can do it on their own end up obsessed with measuring their own moral muscle but never get around to exercising it in real life. Those who trust God's action in them find that God's Spirit is in them—living and breathing God! Obsession with self in these matters is a dead end; attention to God leads us out into the open, into a spacious, free life."

Romans 8:5-8

The original plan for this book was to publish it before my second trip to Everest and to carry a copy to the summit. As we approached the publishing date, my publisher called and convinced me to wait until after the trip to finish the book. In his words..."There's one more chapter."

He was right.

The story of my return to Everest started three years earlier, in 2021, on my descent from my first trip. By the time I reached Kathmandu, I was convinced that I would return. When I called Melanie and the kids, they didn't bat an eye. They were 100% behind a return trip.

That's significant because each of these climbs strains our family. Melanie is a single mom for weeks or months, the kids are without a dad while I'm gone, and each trip puts a financial strain on the family, not to mention the very real possibility that I might not come back alive. I would not have returned to Everest without their enthusiastic support and encouragement.

Everything about the run-up to this trip was unreasonable...

The year before the trip, 2023, was a terrible year financially. Not what you want before committing to a hugely expensive expedition.

I had major foot surgery in September of 2023. In November, I fell off a ladder, breaking both wrists and thumbs. The final surgery to repair my thumbs was in January 2024, just three months before I was scheduled to leave for Everest.

I never fully healed, and the recovery from the surgeries prevented me from doing much of the training I'd planned (and needed) before this trip.

All of that was on top of my everyday struggle with asthma.

Looking at my circumstances, it was utterly unreasonable to believe this trip to Everest was possible.

Living in the 7 Pillars

At the start of this trip, I committed to intentionally living in the 7 Pillars God gave me on my journey to the 7 Summits. Knowing them and living in them are very different things.

Had I not made that commitment, I would not have completed this trip and may not have survived it. Yet, I believe that when we are aligned with our purpose and live in the 7 Pillars, we can push through our circumstances to achieve unreasonable things.

- **Purpose**
- **Death**
- **Obedience**
- **Rest**
- **Relationship**
- **Joy**
- **Manna**

Along the way, **I discovered that conviction in your purpose is paramount. Commitment to lean into the suffering (and there**

will be suffering if you're going to accomplish big things) is necessary. Death to self is essential to make the sacrifice required to grow into who you are really meant to be.

Earlier in the book, I make the case that more is available to you if you want it. Many people never reach even a quarter of their potential. We are meant for more; you are meant for more, but it requires conviction, commitment, and sacrifice. Living in the 7 Pillars is how you do it. This story is my case study for living in the pillars.

Chaos from the Start

Chaos was the rule right from the start of this trip. Yes, there were chaotic events during my earlier climbs–some caused by the people I encountered and the conditions on the mountains, and some caused by me and my inexperience–but this trip was different. Chaos was there at every turn.

I went in with a plan–a detailed timeline I'd built in a spreadsheet–and I also knew that the timeline would be altered. Each change came with a decision–do I continue forward, pivot, or retreat?

The problem with decisions in an environment like Everest is that they are never easy, and you're rarely in the best frame of mind or physical condition to think clearly. Poor decision-making is the #1 cause of death on a climb. Sometimes, it's the decisions made before getting to the mountain or in the lower elevations. Other times, it's the moment-by-moment decisions made at altitude (with far too little oxygen for clear thinking).

For me, this climb's story is a story of decisions and an approach I've come to call **"rigid flexibility."**

My trip started in New York. From there, I flew to Dubai and then to Kathmandu. I landed in Kathmandu in the afternoon, and within a few hours, I was on the move to climb Mera Peak, where the Everest preparation began.

I was scheduled to fly to Lukla from Kathmandu–the main, though primitive, airport gateway to South Side Everest and unlimited hiking routes, but bad weather caused flight cancellations. Companies and people were changing their flights from Kathmandu to Lukla to Ramechhap to Lukla. Flights originating from Ramechhap airport require a very long and undesirable five-hour drive in a taxi over rough terrain…decision point #1.

People were getting sick on these taxi rides, and the opportunity for some other unforeseen problem was high. I said, "No way, I'm not doing that." I chose to roll the dice and wait for a plane that could get me directly to Tenzing-Hillary Airport in Lukla. Leveraging some of my relationships in Kathmandu, I finally got a direct flight, and while I was sitting on the plane, I looked out at the luggage crew and thought to myself… "I don't see my bag."

I had committed to intentionally living in the 7 Pillars through the entire trip, so I said to myself, "Just trust. It's fine."

When we landed in Lukla, there was no bag, no climbing gear, nothing. That was March 22nd, 2024.

Trust.

I waited for two days in Lukla before my gear arrived. It was to my good fortune. The weather was bad those two days. Had I started hiking when I landed, I would have been hiking for two days in the cold and rain. On the way to Mera Peak, there are no hotels like the ones we understand in the West. I stayed in "off the beaten path" tea houses–some were more like the tree houses and forts we built as kids…not usually a warm or comfortable place to stay.

While waiting in Lukla, I met some locals and formed some great relationships that I would have missed otherwise.

Trust.

Getting Acclimated on Mera Peak

As soon as the gear arrived, I headed out for Mera Peak. At 6,476 meters/21,246 feet above sea level, it is the highest trekking (meaning you hike rather than technical climb) mountain in the world, even though we use ice axes, crampons, and climbing gear on summit day.

Because of its high altitude, it's a great place to prepare for Everest. From Lukla, Mera peak is typically a 15- to 20-day trek, and the weather wasn't looking good. I knew I had a small window of opportunity to get up to altitude and prepare my lungs and body for the altitude of Everest.

It was just me and a sherpa, and we were moving fast but cautiously because I didn't want to risk compromising my main objective–summiting the North Side of Everest. It was icy and slick, and I was not a happy camper. This was supposed to be a low-risk trek, but due to the weather conditions, it had turned into a high-risk situation.

I was able to identify a break in the bad weather, and we summited Mera Peak on a beautiful clear, cold day–March 28th, 2024–turned around, and got down and back to Lukla in two days. In total, we did the trek in just seven days, which is unheard of, and headed back to Kathmandu.

Trouble in Kathmandu

When I arrived in Kathmandu, I was fortunate to stay in one of the best hotels in town. I spent a week there working, recovering, and preparing for Everest. At the end of the week, I was scheduled to meet my expedition logistics operator for the Everest climb and head out.

More chaos...

Near the end of the week in Kathmandu, I got food poisoning. The worst food poisoning I've ever experienced. Here, I was supposed to be recovering, and I was actually getting weaker just before I left for Everest.

Let go...trust.

The Complicated Business of Climbing in China

On April 10th, 2024 I had a helicopter scheduled to take me to the Chinese-Nepalese border. Nothing about getting into China or getting approval to climb the Chinese side of Everest is easy.

The Chinese government doesn't want the bad press that comes with accidents and deaths on the mountain–unlike the Nepalese side, where greed and corruption often lead to ill-prepared or inexperienced adventure seekers being pushed up the mountain and either needing rescue or dying on the climb.

To climb in China, you must be approved as a qualified climber and invited to climb. You must obtain a permit from the Chinese-Tibetan Mountaineering Association (CTMA). The permit then goes to the Chinese government and must be signed off. Next, you need a visa to enter China, and on the visa, there must be a note that authorizes you to enter Tibet. Without all the right pieces in place, you're just not getting into the country.

By April 10th, it was clear that my paperwork wouldn't be ready. I needed to pivot.

I decided to go to Langtang, an area just south of the Chinese border in Nepal. Langtang is an area of mountains 40 miles west of Kathmandu where I could trek up to an elevation of roughly 5,500 meters/18,000 feet. There is a great trail system in the area and a number of climbs, which allowed me to keep my body moving and maintain the acclimation I had started at Mera Peak.

I was there for 10 days and ran into several other climbing groups, including a group of old friends who were also preparing for Everest.

We heard from the CTMA that the approval letters would be issued on April 21st, so I headed back to Kathmandu, where I could fulfill any additional requirements the Chinese government might put as conditions for entry into Tibet.

My operator–the climbing company I contracted with–was the only operator with people in Tibet at this time. This was a huge advantage for me. Their team in Tibet was already placing equipment and setting up base camp on Everest by April 19th. We were the only team with a camp on Everest at this point, so I could move fast once I got into Tibet.

"Keep the dream alive."

Every time I spoke with the owner of my operating company, that was our mantra: "Keep the dream alive." Some teams were leaving and going home, giving up on their dreams.

Others were pivoting to climb the South Side of Everest, where I climbed in 2021. The additional teams were creating a tremendous, compounding strain on the already stretched-thin local infrastructure and dangerous congestion on the South Side of the mountain.

Climbers were stuck for hours in long "congo lines," moving up and down the mountain, and people died as a result.

I chose to trust, keep faith, and stay the course.

The 21st came and went, and no letters approving me (or any North Side Everest climbers) to enter China and climb arrived. On April 23rd, China announced that there would be no climbing permits issued for Shishapangma, another 8,000 m. peak in Tibet. Many North-Side climbers assumed there would be a similar announcement for Everest and either canceled their expeditions or changed their plans to climb the South Side of Everest via Nepal.

The Ama Dablam Pivot

I couldn't just sit in a hotel and wait. I needed to keep moving and continue to climb to altitude. I told my operator I wanted to climb Ama Dablam, a 6,812-meter/22,349 feet peak about 9 miles south of Everest in Nepal. Ama Dablam is a difficult and extremely technical high-altitude climb.

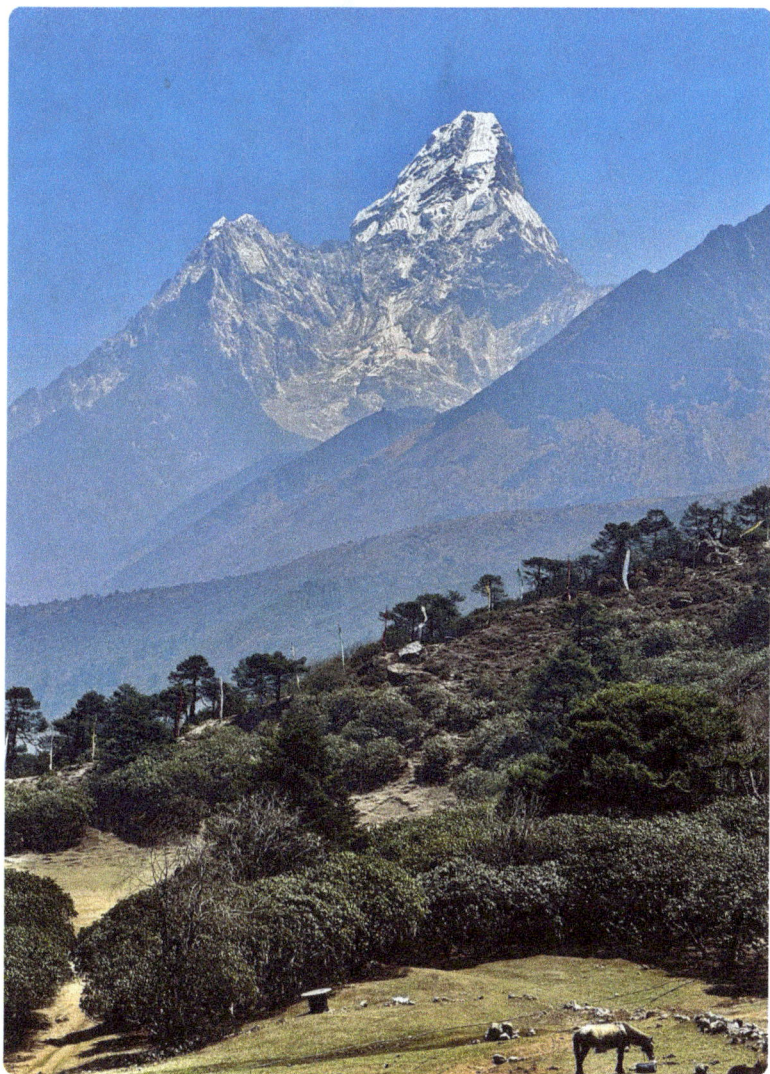

My operator was gracious enough to split the cost of the Ama Dablam climb with me. I was climbing on my own as a self-guided solo climber, without the support of a team, and I was forced to make decisions and advocate for myself on the mountain.

As I was sitting in Camp 2 on Ama Dablam, two support sherpas wanted to push for the summit. I didn't think the conditions were right for a summit push. Leaving at this point would put us on a long exposed ridge to the summit at night and in 60-mile-per-hour winds. Instead, we moved up to Camp 3 the next day and waited. The following day, conditions improved, and we summited. It had turned out to be the right decision–the sherpas thanked me.

These kinds of decisions happen every day on a trip like this–often several times a day and, in some cases, minute by minute.

Being grounded in the 7 Pillars kept me calm and focused while communicating confidence as I stood my ground, knowing that the decision was right for me.

Climbing Through Illness

At the start of the Ama Dablam climb, I was already feeling sick, and I started my "mountain-style" breathing treatments for asthma. By the time I reached Camp 2 and Camp 3, I was significantly worse, with a heavy cough and difficulty breathing. I still felt strong and did not feel as though I compromised myself or others.

On the way down, I started getting extremely sick. It took 16 hours to move from Camp 3 to the summit, and back to base camp. By the time I reached base camp at 4,600 meters/15,091 feet, my lungs were filling with fluid, and my asthma flared up–I could hardly breathe and was gasping for air.

I didn't sleep at all that night. The next day, I made the 13-mile hike out, still sick and struggling to breathe.

I stayed in Namche Bazar overnight but couldn't eat anything. The next morning, I was curled up in a ball on a helipad, waiting for the return flight to Kathmandu. Once settled in at the hotel, I made my way to the hospital.

After a slew of tests, breathing treatments, new asthma meds, a double dose of asthma steroids, and a double dose of antibiotics, I left the hospital. My chances of climbing Everest should have ended there.

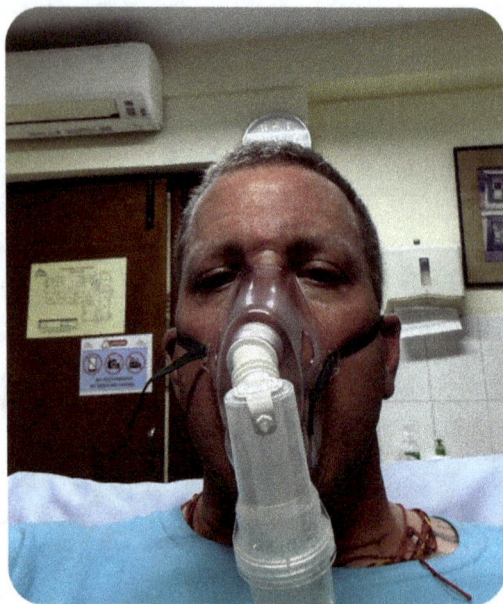

When I returned to Colorado after the trip, I met with a sports medicine doctor who was shocked that I could continue after this episode on the mountain.

I stayed aligned to my purpose and continued to work within my risk management plan. Hour by hour, I told myself, "I can do anything for one more hour,"...then, "I can do anything for one more day."

I stayed in Kathmandu for two days, and I could feel God working in me. Gradually, I regained enough strength to move on to the next step.

Green Light to Everest

On May 7th, I received my letter granting permission to enter Tibet and make the climb. On May 9th, I was in a helicopter flying to Timure on the Tibetan (Chinese) border.

Having my invitation letter was one thing. Actually getting into Tibet was another. There are so many layers of bureaucracy, each one political, and every move you make is under the close scrutiny of the Chinese government. You can feel the weight of it all.

To cross the border, you go through several checkpoints–guards at each. We entered one building, and in front of us, people were being turned around and denied entry. After everything I had been through, it was enough to make me nervous.

Then, there was a health screening. After being so sick, I still had a latent cough. I was downing cough drops like candy to keep from coughing. I didn't want to appear sick and give them any excuse for sending me back to Nepal.

Then, they screen your phone–particularly looking for pictures of the Dali Lama. Any image of him on my phone–even as little as a portrait hanging on a wall in the background of one of my photos–would be enough to deny my entry to Tibet.

Next, they put you through an interview–really more of an inter-rogation. Throughout the process, there are cameras everywhere–you are being watched.

When I finally made it through, I took a deep breath. Just to get to this point, I relied on a string of little miracles.

From the border, a group of us headed to a town called Tingri. We arrived close to midnight, and we were brought into this tiny restaurant and seated in the corner. The restaurant was dark–no electricity because the power grid isn't always reliable–and we didn't know what was happening. Then, the owners brought us plates of amazing Chinese food. It was our first opportunity to relax for a moment.

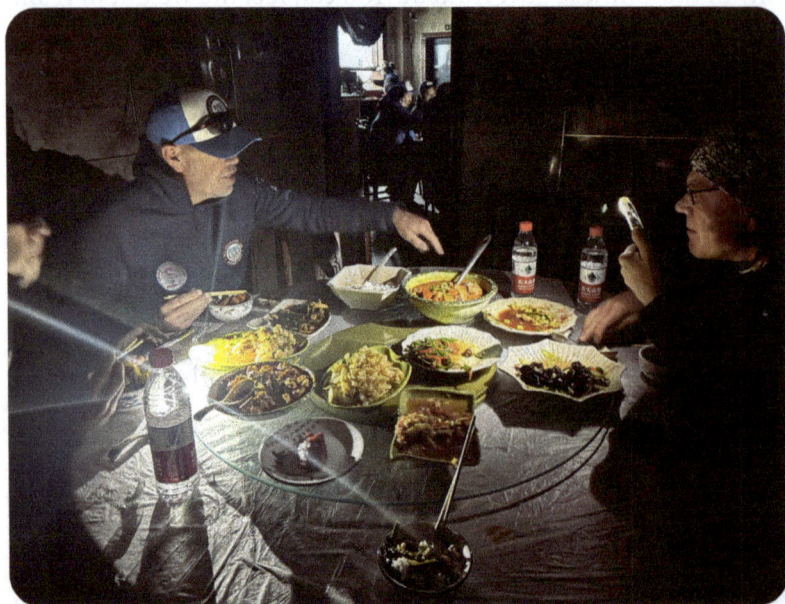

I ate, rested, and prayed for two days in Tingri while finishing my meds. It's amazing what a couple of days of rest in a comfortable bed will do for you. Miraculously, I was feeling much better.

We arrived at Everest Base Camp on May 11th–my wife Melanie's birthday–after a 3-hour drive from Tingri. You could feel the excitement. We're finally here. It's time to climb.

Everest Base Camp

Time to Climb

On May 16th, we left Everest Base Camp and headed for Intermediate Camp at 5,800 meters/19,000 feet. The goal was to stay there overnight and acclimate to the altitude. I planned to move to Advanced Base Camp with three other climbers, a 13–mile hike from Base Camp.

By the time we arrived at Advanced Base Camp, I was in miserable shape again. My head was pounding (which is normal during acclimatization, but at this point, I should have been fully acclimatized from my climbs in Nepal), and I was sick. Advanced Base Camp is at 6,400 meters/21,000 feet – an altitude humans aren't meant to operate at.

Physical suffering is part of climbing. I don't like it; no climber does, but we are operating at altitudes that the human body was not designed for. Add to that extreme cold and the extreme physical strain of climbing, and you will face suffering.

The question is, how will you deal with the suffering? Will you be Bigger than the suffering, or will it overtake you? For me, I put my trust in Him–something infinitely larger than the suffering. I continued to live in the 7 Pillars, which gave me a calm confidence that I know was essential to my survival.

We stayed at Advanced Base Camp for two days, and the entire time, I was trying to get weather reports and make decisions about when I would attempt the summit. My communications unit broke while being transported to Advanced Base Camp by a yak.

Yaks carrying our equipment.

At one point, I was inside a rickety communications tent on a Chinese team's radio with a Nepalese translator, gathering weather data at base camp and relaying it in Nepalese to my sherpa, who translated it into English. Talk about a game of telephone!

My operator and I disagreed about when to attempt the summit. Being a self-guided expedition, the final decision was always mine, but as a leader, I knew I needed my support team to be fully aligned.

The weather looked good on May 21st and 22nd. And the rule on Everest is that when the weather is good, storms are not far behind. I really wanted to make the summit push on the 21st or 22nd, but there was a problem.

The Chinese have a law that requires Chinese climbers to have the opportunity to summit before everyone else. In Advanced Base

Camp and throughout the climb, I was constantly talking with the Chinese climbing team and the Chinese-Tibetan Mountaineering Association, trying to find out when they were going up and pushing to be right there with them.

The Chinese were having none of it. I wanted to go behind them on the 23rd. I knew the weather was likely to turn on the 27th–the date my operator was pushing for. I agreed to adjust my summit approach and plan to wait on a better forecast for the 27th summit.

From Advanced Base Camp, I headed to North Col at 7,000 meters/23,000 feet. The North Col of Everest sits at 23,000 feet above sea level–**higher than anything outside the Himalayas. Yet, this is barely the starting point for the climb to the summit at 29,031 feet.**

Climb High, Sleep Low

Typical climbing practice is to climb to a higher altitude to acclimate your body to lower oxygen levels at higher altitude, then return to a lower altitude (sometimes just a few thousand feet lower, sometimes all the way off the mountain).

By going down to a lower altitude, your body has an opportunity to recover from the stress caused by the lower oxygen levels higher up. Recovery is important. It is where you build the capacity to go even higher.

We now had reports suggesting significantly unfavorable weather after the 23rd. Rather than return to a lower altitude, I stayed at North Col for two days. This aligned with my original plan to summit on the 23rd. This goes against common climbing practice and conventional wisdom. Climbers reading this might think I was being irresponsible, but I knew that if I took the time to go lower and recover, I would get little to no recovery down at 21,000 ft because of the reduced lung capacity caused by my illness and asthma and going down and climbing back up to North Col would expend a huge amount of energy. It was a judgment call. I knew that if I went down to Advanced Base Camp, I would miss the weather window, and I wouldn't have an opportunity to summit.

Before I left home for this trip, I built a detailed risk management plan. For each leg of the journey, I had pre-determined my go/no-go criteria. I was still within my "go" parameters, so the decision, though unconventional, was clear–continue for the 3-day summit push from North Col.

The first Chinese team summited as scheduled on May 21st, with the second reaching the summit on May 22nd. That cleared the way for me to summit on May 23rd.

My sherpa–Pemba–and I left Camp 3 for the summit. I was still nowhere near 100 percent, but I felt strong, and I continually–hour by hour–assessed my condition. My lung capacity was diminished from my asthma and the illness a few days earlier–not a great way to be when you're at 23,000 feet and going to 29,000 feet.

I didn't have my summit gear because I stayed at North Col rather than going back down to Advanced Base Camp before the summit push. I didn't have my summit kit including medicines, food, cameras or batteries. My watch had died. And I didn't have my fresh summit layers or my summit headlamp. We also had a limited supply of oxygen available above North Col–just three bottles of oxygen for me and two for Pemba. That was enough, but we didn't have any redundancy.

When pushing from Advanced Base Camp through the high camps and to the summit, most climbers will set their oxygen flow to 2 liters per hour and increase as needed every few thousand feet of altitude up to 8 liters per hour. Moving at a strong and controlled pace allows plenty of "oxygen time" to make it to the summit and back.

I wasn't moving at a normal pace. I was slower. I figured that with my reduced lung capacity, flowing at 4 liters per hour would deplete my oxygen, so I climbed at a reduced flow of just 2 liters per hour. This gave me twice as much "oxygen time" and helped compensate for my lack of extra oxygen bottles but could not make up for my limited lung capacity.

The other variable I was weighing was my total exposure time at altitude. At these high altitudes, your body is only depleting. There is no recovery. Digestion slows. Your body is effectively shutting down because it's not getting enough oxygen into all of your tissues.

Without my summit kit, I had only a small bag of rice to eat to last me the next several days. At that altitude, your body doesn't really process food, but by the time I reached the summit, I'd been four days without real food and six or seven days without sleep.

Moving to the Summit

From Advanced Base Camp, you move to the high camps, which are stops along the way to adjust, prepare, and recover as best as possible. At this altitude, most climbers sleep on oxygen (if they sleep at all).

Being up this high is dangerous. The lack of oxygen causes your body to slowly stop functioning. Your body is not processing the food you eat, so your body survives by eating itself. Between my earlier illness and the climb itself, I lost 13.6 kg./30 lbs.

I reached High Camp 2 and stopped there. I was in a tent, and a sherpa came to the tent and asked if someone could share the tent with me. My first reaction was no, absolutely not. I didn't want to risk getting sicker. Then, a Norwegian climber poked his head in, and I recognized him from a few days earlier. I waved him in. It was great to have a little conversation while we rested.

We got along well and ended up moving to Camp 3 together. At Camp 3, I don't know what happened, how to explain it, or what it means. I got highly emotional… I was reading messages on my satellite communicator, and I realized this was the last "what if" of the trip. From here, I was headed to the summit.

Summit or Not - Pros and Cons

A week before I arrived at Everest Base Camp, I made a list of the pros and cons of summiting versus not summiting Everest. Since my climb on the South Side in 2021, I have been haunted by the question that everyone asks when you say you've climbed Everest: "Did you summit?"

I was at peace with our decision not to summit in 2021. It protected the lives of our sherpas, and it was the right decision. People who have never been on an expedition like this only see the summit. Yet, those who have climbed know that the summit is a snapshot. The journey is where all the danger, struggle, and suffering are endured.

I've learned that being **convicted in your goal, committing to it, enduring the suffering and sacrifice necessary to reach the goal** through the journey are where you learn who you really are, what you are truly capable of, and where significant growth happens.

I completed my analysis and concluded that there was no upside to stopping short of the summit. I had my risk management plan and was committed to staying within it. If I didn't make it due to circumstances on the mountain, I was OK with it.

Yes, it would mean losing all the money invested in the trip...losing the time...going through the suffering without reaching the goal... returning to the same question: "Did you summit?" with the same answer: "No."

Having clarity on the reasons for doing something big is essential fuel for persevering through the stuffing of the journey.

On the night of May 22nd, it was time to leave for the summit. For the first time, Pemba and I were climbing together. To this point, I went ahead, and he joined me at each camp after I arrived. Chinese law requires that climbers be accompanied by a sherpa on summit day so that there is an experienced pair of eyes observing and ready to assist when issues arise (and they always do). We left late at night, approximately midnight. This part of the journey is extremely steep. I hadn't eaten or slept in days. I was tired, and I couldn't breathe. I didn't want to go. Emotionally, I didn't care about the summit anymore–which is not like me at all.

At that point, it seemed as if God removed the world from me... he removed the "Scott" from me and gave me a focus. I had tied a blue face covering that I'd purchased in Kathmandu around my arm on the outside of my 8,000-meter suit. That blue band became my focus. It represented my "why"–Kingdom impact. Always in my field of view, it fueled my resolve to take one more step.

Given my lowered lung capacity, I couldn't move at my normal pace. I calculated that I would be 20% to 30% slower.

This is where the risk management plan paid off. I had already divided the summit push into five timed milestones from Camp 3.

1. Camp 3 to 1st Step: 8,500 meters/27,890 feet - 2 hours
2. 1st Step to Mushroom Rock: 8,549 meters/28,047 feet - 1 hour
3. Mushroom Rock to 2nd Step: 8,577 meters/28,140 feet - 2 hours
4. 2nd Step to 3rd Step: 8,690 meters/28,500 feet - 2 hours
5. 3rd Step to Summit: 8,849 meters/29,031 feet - 2.5 hours

Each time was the maximum allowable time. If I didn't make a milestone within the max time, it was a non-negotiable decision to turn around.

At each milestone, I did a quick assessment:

- Am I cold?
- Can I feel my toes? Are they cold?
- Can I feel my fingers? Are they cold?
- Do I have a headache?
- Is my vision compromised?
- Do I seem to be thinking logically?
- Do I know my name?
- Do I know where I am?
- Can I do simple math in my head?
- Am I able to physically function?

Fingers and toes...the body's early warning system

I'm sure you've been out in winter weather and said, "I'm so cold." I did, too. Then, I discovered what cold on Everest is...real, true, life-threatening cold. Average temperatures at the summit during the peak climbings month of May are -13° to -17°F. Add to that winds that are often blowing at 150 miles per hour, and you have a cold, unlike anything most humans experience.

The fingers and toes are the early warning that you're getting into danger. As you lose feeling in your fingers and toes, you're in the beginning stages of frostbite. When your core body temperature gets too low, your body begins to reduce circulation to the extremities in an all-out effort to keep your vital organs warm and keep you alive.

Keeping a close awareness of your fingers and toes is essential to managing risk in the extreme cold of Everest.

If you remember, my watch had died because I chose to stay at North Col and not return to Advanced Base Camp due to weather window and the cost benefit of energy expenditure vs. potential recovery at 21,000 ft vs. 23,000 ft. Traveling at night, I estimated the time by the position of the moon, and I was able to look at my phone with about 10% battery life during a short break about halfway up.

I reached Step 1, and it required big movements to climb over large boulders. It takes a lot of strength and energy.

About an hour later, I got to Step 2. Step 2 is highly technical. You have to climb a series of ladders, one of which is a nearly vertical 30-foot climb on rickety Chinese ladders. We're very high at this point, and it's a 12,000-foot drop. Any mistake, and you're dead.

And I loved every minute of it. I had fun. The technical aspect engaged my mind because you have to think through every move–step here, clip onto the correct rope, move. Very little smart or fast thinking happens at this altitude, but I was encouraged by having a test for my logical brain and discovering it was still sharp.

From there, we moved to Step 3. Each of these steps is a place in the route where you make a vertical climb. I got to Step 3 and thought, "Oh great, another one." I made it up one side and looked up, and there was the summit snowfield and summit ridge to battle before finally seeing the last push to the top of the world.

It looked so close, yet we were still about two hours away.

Approaching the summit ridge, I expected a nice, easy slope to the summit. It was nothing but steep, all the way. As you reach the top, there are three small ledges you have to climb to get to the summit itself.

When I reached the top, it was the strangest feeling. I didn't have the euphoria you would expect. I "checked the box," I did it…now let's get down.

The Descent–Facing Death

Leaving the summit, the first challenge is getting through the three steps. Step 3 is now first. Just past Step 3 in the middle of an ice storm, Pemba pointed at my left boot and freaked out… "Where is your crampon?!" We were stuck in knee-deep snow and there was no chance to successfully descend without the crampon.

I suggested to Pemba that the crampon must have come off while climbing down the rock on step 3. I have never lost a crampon before or ever had one pop-off. This was serious. Pemba gave me his crampon and told me to hurry down without him. There was no way I was leaving him. So Pemba went back to Step 3 to search and I searched in the snow where we were.

Twenty minutes later, Pemba appeared with the missing crampon. We headed down, cheating death for the moment.

Zombie Death

More climbers die on the descent than on the climb. You're depleted physically, mentally, and emotionally. It's easy to make mistakes or simply give up.

I have seen videos of climbers just stopping and sitting down on the descent, but I never understood it until this point of the trip. I was struggling physically as we left the summit and headed to Camp 3.

As we were moving down, I wanted to stop and sit down in fresh, white, fluffy snow for a short break. I was completely calm, and it was a very peaceful moment. I looked out at the vastness and realized… there is no one coming for me. There is no one in sight. It's just Pemba and me on this part of the mountain. There is no rescue. There is no help.

That's what's very different between the North Side of Everest and the South Side. On the South Side, people are everywhere; there are long lines, and there are many teams. People who would otherwise die on the mountain can be helicoptered off or given words of encouragement to push on to safety.

On the North Side, especially this year, we were on our own. I was one of just 12 foreign climbers to summit the North Side in 2024…it's a big, lonely, dangerous mountain. However, this year was a privilege to be in the purity and authenticity of what early mountaineers may have experienced.

At this point, I knew I still had my logical mind because I reasoned with myself: "If I sit, I'm going to die…and I don't want to die, so I'm going to keep going."

I cheated death again.

When we reached Camp 3, I found some noodles to eat in one of the tents left behind by the Chinese. It wasn't much, but it was something. Pemba made some hot tea for me, which was amazing.

You can't stay in Camp 3; it's too elevated, and the opportunity for death is very high. At this point, I stayed at North Col on the ascent longer than normal and had far too much high-altitude exposure. We needed to get down out of the death zone.

My initial goal was to descend to Advanced Base Camp on summit day. We weren't going to make it that far. However, I knew we needed to push on to Camp 2 at 7,700 meters/25,200 feet. I was in bad shape. My lungs were trashed. We stayed in Camp 2 overnight. I couldn't sleep but needed some recovery. My lungs were full of mucus, and laying down would have led to suffocation. I had so much trouble breathing due to asthma. Pemba and I radioed down to Advanced Base Camp, and these amazing people sent a porter up with my medkit and an oxygen cylinder for me.

Unable to get into my sleeping bag, I just wrapped it around me, stayed on oxygen, and focused on making it through the night.

I started taking nifedipine to treat High-Altitude Pulmonary Edema (HAPE).

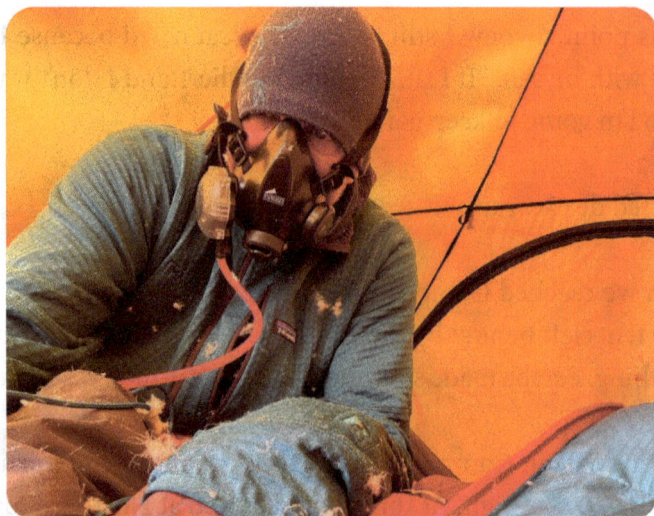

When the sun came up in the morning, we were on the move, and I knew I needed to get to Advanced Base Camp today if I was going to survive. We reached the camp at North Col and rested there for an hour, then continued to Advanced Base Camp. I was actually able to enjoy repelling and climbing down from North Col to Advanced Base Camp and take in the beauty.

We reached Advanced Base Camp, and I tested my blood oxygen saturation using Pulse Oximetry, and it was 85, which is good. In my mind, this ruled out HAPE. I was confident that my difficulty breathing and all the other symptoms I was feeling were a result of my asthma and lingering illness. I spent the night in Advanced Base Camp on oxygen because I just wasn't getting any air through my beat-up lungs.

The next day, we had to make the 13-mile trek to Base Camp. If you're suffering from altitude sickness, the best thing you can do to get better is go lower. For me, the lower I went, the worse I got.

I was terribly sick on the hike. We hit the intermediate camp about halfway between Advanced Base Camp and Base Camp, and I really wanted to stop and stay there. Pemba pushed me. The Chinese were tearing down the tents, and he said, "There's no place to stay. We're moving."

On we went—seven more miles to Base Camp.

I am so thankful that he pushed me.

Base Camp sounds comforting, and it is, but it is still at an elevation of 17,000 ft. For perspective, pilots are required to be on supplemental oxygen when flying above 12,500 feet (if they don't have a pressurized cabin). At 17,000 feet, your body is getting very little recovery. You're still oxygen-deprived.

We reached Base Camp, and my support team was there, excited to see me. This was a significant moment—not just for me, but for everyone involved. Since China had been closed to foreign climbers for years, being the first American to summit since 2019 was a big deal. The Chinese authorities and Climbalaya, the only Nepali operator allowed on the North Side of Everest in 2024, were particularly invested in this climb.

At Base Camp, I was honored with the presentation of a Kata, a traditional white scarf that is commonly given as a blessing in Tibetan Buddhism. While Katas are often exchanged in Nepal, receiving one from the Chinese government is a rare and profound sign of respect. The woman presenting it was part of the CTMA (Chinese Tibetan Mountaineering Association), underscoring the importance of this moment. We celebrated, got some rest, and stayed at Base Camp for two additional days before the 10-hour drive to Kyirong to stay the night.

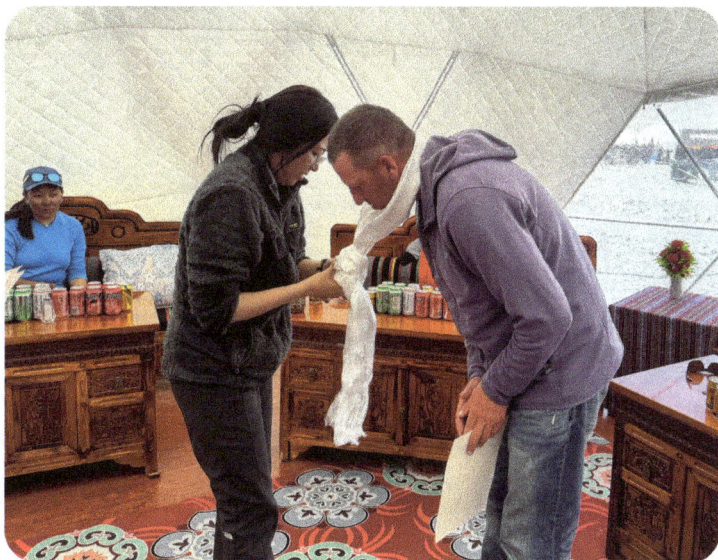

For this leg of the journey, I traveled with a British father-son team who had summited just after me on the 24th and my good friend Francois from France. From there, we got the permits needed to cross the border back into Nepal.

At Timure, Nepal, we could not get the permit for a helicopter to land. So we drove 13 miles East to Langtang. In Langtang, the British father found an old tea house for us to relax in, and they had beers that must have been 20 years old. Those may have been the best beers we ever had. It was a great moment to exhale and relax.

From Langtang to Kathmandu and home.

Conviction - Commitment - Sacrifice

There is more available to you. You are capable of reaching it. Are you willing to be convicted in your purpose? Are you willing to commit to lean into the suffering? Are you willing to die to yourself to sacrifice what is necessary to reach your goal and be aligned with your intended purpose?

If you are not convicted in your purpose, you may fail to reach your goal.

Are you willing to take action? Are you willing to sacrifice?

Throughout this journey to Everest, I stayed convicted in my purpose–to connect with others for Kingdom Impact. I was committed to the goal–summit the North Side of Everest. I was willing to sacrifice and endure suffering to see it through.

I'm not special. I could not do that on my own, and that's the point.

I lived the 7 Pillars and applied them to my decision-making. By living intentionally every day in the 7 Pillars, I was able to keep going even when there was suffering and uncertainty, and the possibility of success looked bleak.

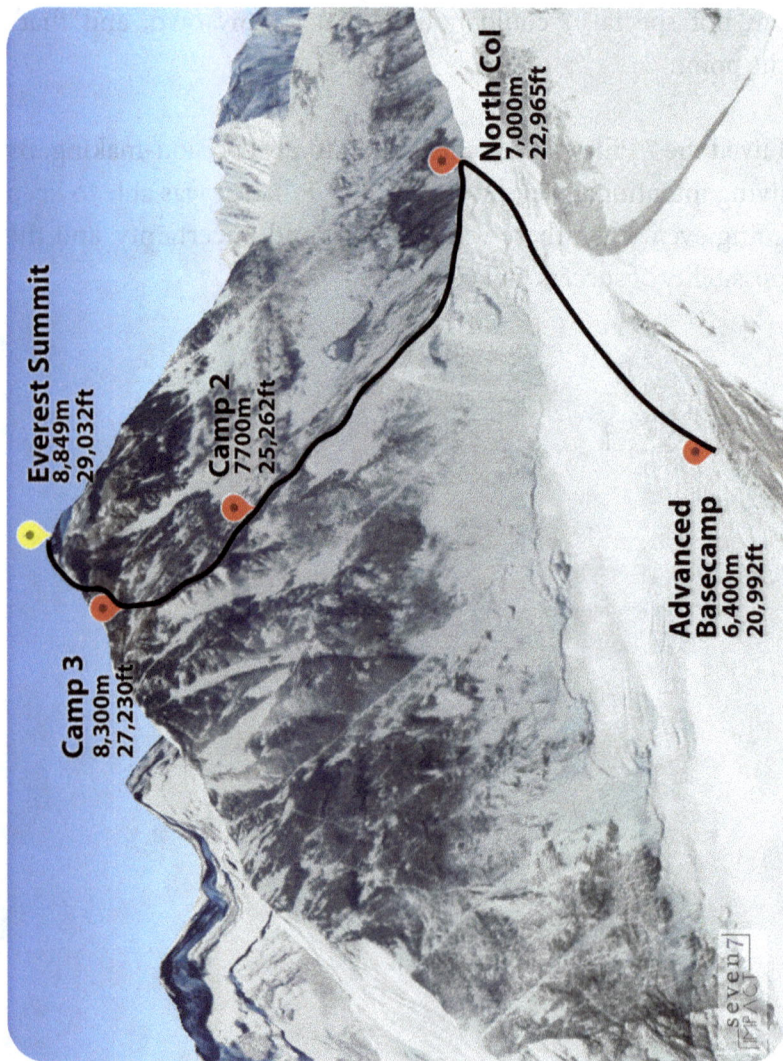

North Col
7,000m
22,965ft

Everest Summit
8,849m
29,032ft

Camp 2
7700m
25,262ft

Camp 3
8,300m
27,230ft

Advanced Basecamp
6,400m
20,992ft

seven7

EVEREST 2024

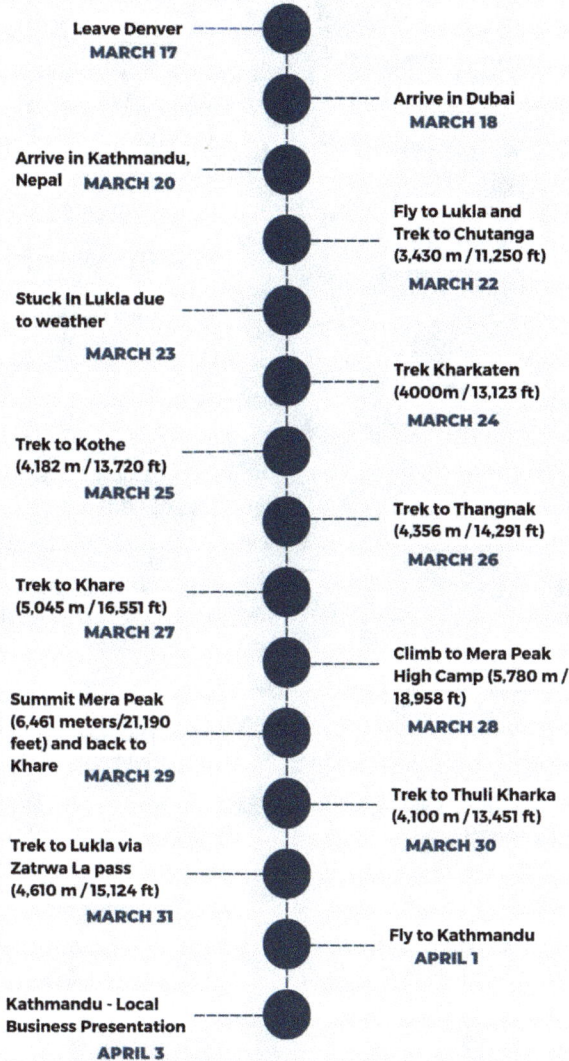

Leave Denver
MARCH 17

Arrive in Dubai
MARCH 18

Arrive in Kathmandu,
Nepal **MARCH 20**

Fly to Lukla and
Trek to Chutanga
(3,430 m / 11,250 ft)
MARCH 22

Stuck In Lukla due
to weather
MARCH 23

Trek Kharkaten
(4000m / 13,123 ft)
MARCH 24

Trek to Kothe
(4,182 m / 13,720 ft)
MARCH 25

Trek to Thangnak
(4,356 m / 14,291 ft)
MARCH 26

Trek to Khare
(5,045 m / 16,551 ft)
MARCH 27

Climb to Mera Peak
High Camp (5,780 m /
18,958 ft)
MARCH 28

Summit Mera Peak
(6,461 meters/21,190
feet) and back to
Khare **MARCH 29**

Trek to Thuli Kharka
(4,100 m / 13,451 ft)
MARCH 30

Trek to Lukla via
Zatrwa La pass
(4,610 m / 15,124 ft)
MARCH 31

Fly to Kathmandu
APRIL 1

Kathmandu - Local
Business Presentation
APRIL 3

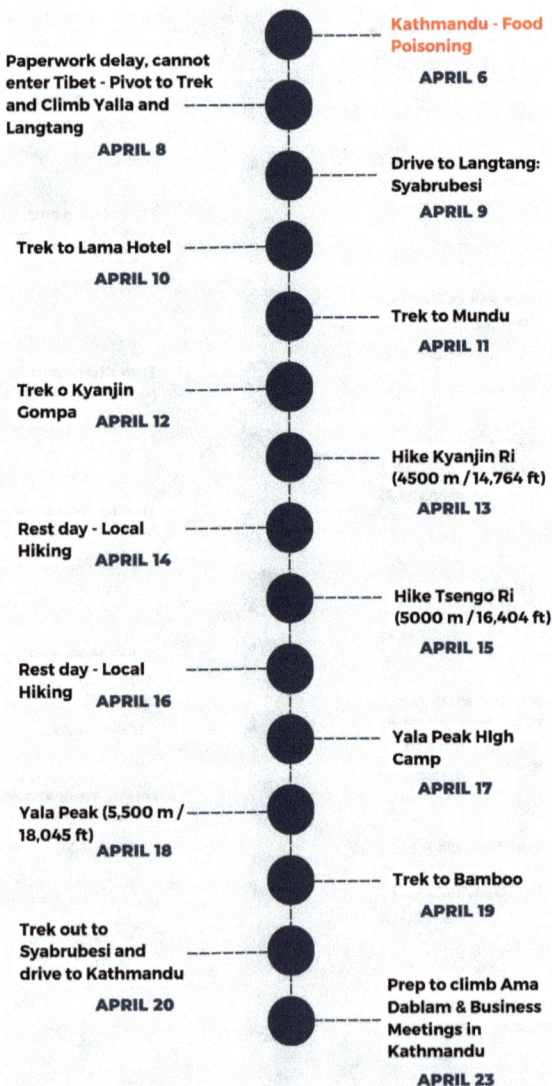

Kathmandu - Food Poisoning
APRIL 6

Paperwork delay, cannot enter Tibet - Pivot to Trek and Climb Yalla and Langtang
APRIL 8

Drive to Langtang: Syabrubesi
APRIL 9

Trek to Lama Hotel
APRIL 10

Trek to Mundu
APRIL 11

Trek o Kyanjin Gompa
APRIL 12

Hike Kyanjin Ri (4500 m / 14,764 ft)
APRIL 13

Rest day - Local Hiking
APRIL 14

Hike Tsengo Ri (5000 m / 16,404 ft)
APRIL 15

Rest day - Local Hiking
APRIL 16

Yala Peak High Camp
APRIL 17

Yala Peak (5,500 m / 18,045 ft)
APRIL 18

Trek to Bamboo
APRIL 19

Trek out to Syabrubesi and drive to Kathmandu
APRIL 20

Prep to climb Ama Dablam & Business Meetings in Kathmandu
APRIL 23

PIVOT TO CLIMB AMA DABLAM TO ACCLIMATE

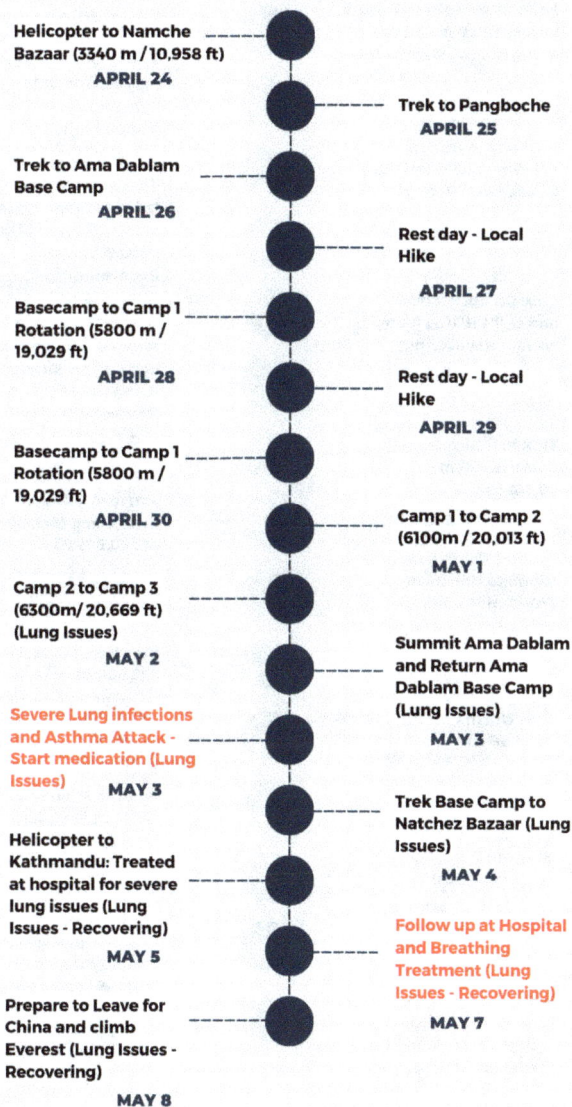

Helicopter to Namche Bazaar (3340 m / 10,958 ft)
APRIL 24

Trek to Pangboche
APRIL 25

Trek to Ama Dablam Base Camp
APRIL 26

Rest day - Local Hike
APRIL 27

Basecamp to Camp 1 Rotation (5800 m / 19,029 ft)
APRIL 28

Rest day - Local Hike
APRIL 29

Basecamp to Camp 1 Rotation (5800 m / 19,029 ft)
APRIL 30

Camp 1 to Camp 2 (6100m / 20,013 ft)
MAY 1

Camp 2 to Camp 3 (6300m/ 20,669 ft) (Lung Issues)
MAY 2

Summit Ama Dablam and Return Ama Dablam Base Camp (Lung Issues)
MAY 3

Severe Lung infections and Asthma Attack - Start medication (Lung Issues)
MAY 3

Trek Base Camp to Natchez Bazaar (Lung Issues)
MAY 4

Helicopter to Kathmandu: Treated at hospital for severe lung issues (Lung Issues - Recovering)
MAY 5

Follow up at Hospital and Breathing Treatment (Lung Issues - Recovering)
MAY 7

Prepare to Leave for China and climb Everest (Lung Issues - Recovering)
MAY 8

PIVOT TO EXIT NEPAL AND ENTER TIBET

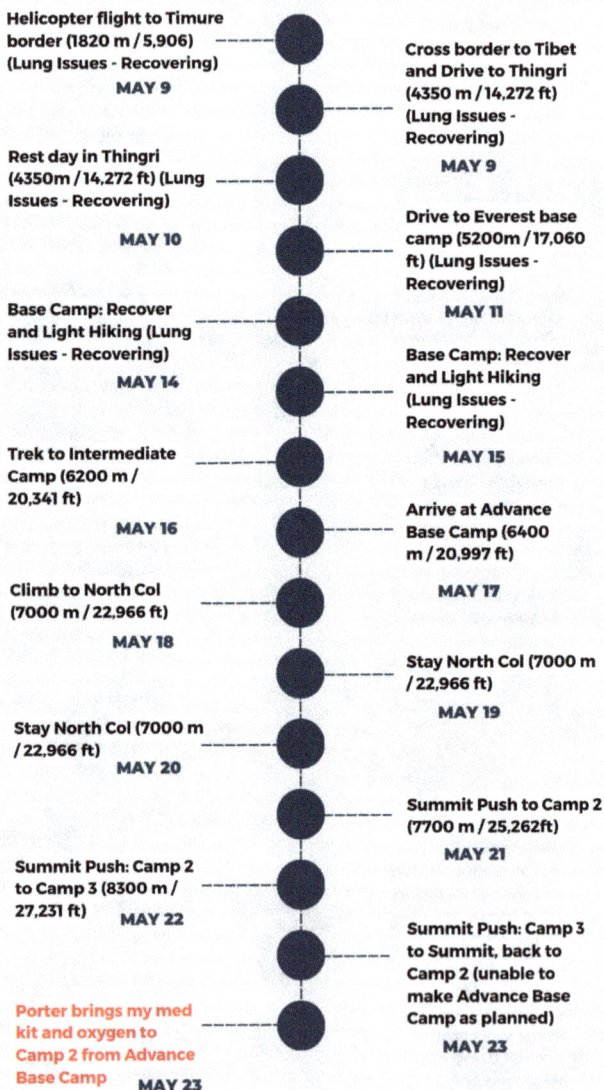

Helicopter flight to Timure border (1820 m / 5,906) (Lung Issues - Recovering)
MAY 9

Cross border to Tibet and Drive to Thingri (4350 m / 14,272 ft) (Lung Issues - Recovering)
MAY 9

Rest day in Thingri (4350m / 14,272 ft) (Lung Issues - Recovering)
MAY 10

Drive to Everest base camp (5200m / 17,060 ft) (Lung Issues - Recovering)
MAY 11

Base Camp: Recover and Light Hiking (Lung Issues - Recovering)
MAY 14

Base Camp: Recover and Light Hiking (Lung Issues - Recovering)
MAY 15

Trek to Intermediate Camp (6200 m / 20,341 ft)
MAY 16

Arrive at Advance Base Camp (6400 m / 20,997 ft)
MAY 17

Climb to North Col (7000 m / 22,966 ft)
MAY 18

Stay North Col (7000 m / 22,966 ft)
MAY 19

Stay North Col (7000 m / 22,966 ft)
MAY 20

Summit Push to Camp 2 (7700 m / 25,262ft)
MAY 21

Summit Push: Camp 2 to Camp 3 (8300 m / 27,231 ft)
MAY 22

Summit Push: Camp 3 to Summit, back to Camp 2 (unable to make Advance Base Camp as planned)
MAY 23

Porter brings my med kit and oxygen to Camp 2 from Advance Base Camp
MAY 23

Advance Base Camp to Base Camp - Climbalaya Celebration for my Summit (5200 m / 17,060 ft)

MAY 25

Camp 2 to Advance Base Camp (6400 m / 20,997 ft)

MAY 24

Chinese Tibetan Mountaineering Association Cermemony at Base Camp

MAY 26

Leave Base Camp - Drive to Kyirong (2700 m / 8,858 ft)

MAY 27

Cross border into Nepal - drive to Langtang - Helicopter to Kathmandu

MAY 28

Kathmandu meetings and rest/recover

MAY 29 - JUNE 2

CONCLUSION

Unreasonable Impact

You've read this far... You might be wondering, "What was the point?"

I believe the point of my journey is this...

That God calls his people.

That we are to be attentive and accountable in listening for the call.

That His ways are not our ways. We may not understand them, and we may be confused by His ask.

We will certainly be told by the world, by the culture, and even by our closest friends that what we heard couldn't possibly be right because it is *unreasonable* to our understanding of the world.

St. Paul says in his Letter to the Romans, Chapter 12, verse 2: *"Do not be conformed to this world, but be transformed by the renewal of your mind, that by testing you may discern what is the will of God, what is good and acceptable and perfect."*

You must test what you hear as your call to determine if it is the will of God. At the beginning of my journey, it took several years for me to discern with confidence that what I'd been asked to do was, in fact, the will of God.

Then, once convinced, embrace *unreasonable obedience.*

This book is not a how-to manual on obedience. It is merely a testimony of what I experienced as a result of choosing obedience—unreasonable obedience.

You will undoubtedly experience other things, maybe greater things than I did.

As I reflect back on my journey, what I now realize is that the call required obedience, and the obedience led to contribution. I became a vessel through which Christ acted in the world. He was in me and acted through me.

I was there, yet I did not act on my own. My only act was the choice to be obedient when called. This was my call to adventure.

God is up to big things in the world, and he wants you to play a role.

Are you <u>willing</u>?

This story is not about seeing the impact and I may never know the full impact that this story unlocks. However, I am confident my obedience will lead to much more than any of us can comprehend.

MY INSIGHTS FROM THE 7 SUMMITS

Kilimanjaro — Purpose

Purpose is clarity about what you're supposed to do. Purpose is the what. When I gained clarity on what I was supposed to do, I experienced greatness. That greatness was the exhilarating goosebumps moment I felt while walking in my purpose. Purpose has had a lasting effect on me, allowing me to connect with people where they are and guide them toward great things.

Elbrus — Death

Death, to me, is about dying to myself every day and letting go of how the world wants me to be. I strive to live each day from my core values and not compromise who I am when making decisions. When I stay true to my personal core values, I operate at full capacity, with clear intentions rooted in knowing who I am.

Mt. Kosciusko — Obedience

Obedience is having faith and taking action. It's about following my belief system. With faith, I have the confidence that my beliefs are strong enough to guide me through. I find inspiration in knowing what I'm supposed to do and letting go of the need for acknowledgment.

Aconcagua — Rest

Rest is confidence in who I am in my belief system. Rest is knowing that I am enough in Christ and that I can find peace knowing He is enough for me.

Denali — Relationship

Relationship is knowing that there's no way I can do this on my own strength and fully surrendering to that fact. This realization opens the door to connecting and sharing with others, leading to even more success and personal fulfillment. I focus on fostering and growing relationships and making choices that strengthen community, culture, and legacy.

Mt. Vinson — Joy

Joy doesn't just happen to me—it's not the same as happiness. It's a state of being joyful in whatever role I find myself in each day. I make a conscious choice to live by these lessons and share that gift with others. I strive to build joy within my teams and avoid letting arrogance and control lead to missteps that could devastate our success.

Everest — Manna

Manna represents being supplied with what I need on a daily basis. With perspective, I can step back and evaluate what I need each day by breaking it down into manageable pieces. When communication from my leaders is unclear, I take charge and have confidence in my ability to move forward.

ABOUT THE AUTHOR

Scott Cutlan, a distinguished international keynote speaker and seasoned executive, serves as the driving force behind activating individuals' greatness through the strategic alignment of their purpose. As an accomplished leader with a background in executive roles, advanced mountaineering, and a commitment to purpose-driven initiatives, Scott focuses on cultivating thriving global communities. He excels at dismantling barriers and instilling empowerment in individuals to authentically live out their intended purpose. Having traversed all 7 continents and visited 85+ countries, Scott establishes impactful relationships. Through the establishment of his non-profit, he is strategically building a global network with the vision and ambition to adeptly transform multicultural challenges into highly impactful solutions.